Counting the People

GW00492935

Maynooth Research Guides for Irish Local History

GENERAL EDITOR Mary Ann Lyons

This book is one of the Maynooth Research Guides for Irish Local History series. Written by specialists in the relevant fields, these volumes are designed to provide historians, and specifically those interested in local history, with practical advice regarding the consultation of specific collections of historical material, thereby enabling them to conduct independent research in a competent and thorough manner. In each volume, a brief history of the relevant institutions is provided and the principal primary sources are identified and critically evaluated, with specific reference to their usefulness to the local historian. Readers receive step by step guidance as to how to conduct their research and are alerted to some of the problems which they might encounter in working with particular collections. Possible avenues for research are suggested and relevant secondary works are also recommended.

The General Editor acknowledges the assistance of both Dr Raymond Gillespie, Co-ordinator of the M.A. in Local History programme, N.U.I. Maynooth and Dr James Kelly, St Patrick's College, Drumcondra, in the preparation of this book for publication.

IN THIS SERIES

Terence A. M. Dooley, *Sources for the history of landed estates in Ireland* (Irish Academic Press, 2000)

Raymond Refaussé, *Church of Ireland records* (Irish Academic Press, 2000)

Patrick J. Corish and David C. Sheehy, *Records of the Irish Catholic Church* (Irish Academic Press, 2001)

Philomena Connolly, *Medieval record sources* (Four Courts Press, 2002)

Brian Gurrin, *Pre-census sources for Irish demography* (Four Courts Press, 2002)

E. Margaret Crawford, *Counting the people: a survey of the Irish censuses, 1813–1911* (Four Courts Press, 2003)

Maynooth Research Guides for Irish Local History: Number 6

Counting the People
A survey of the Irish censuses, 1813–1911

E. Margaret Crawford

FOUR COURTS PRESS

Set in 10.5 pt on 12.5 pt Bembo by
Carrigboy Typesetting Services for
FOUR COURTS PRESS
7 Malpas Street, Dublin 8
e-mail: info@four-courts-press.ie
and in North America by
FOUR COURTS PRESS
c/o ISBS, 920 N.E. 58th Avenue, Suite 300, Portland, OR 97213

A catalogue record for this title
is available from the British Library.

ISBN 1–85182–673–4

Printed and bound in Great Britain by
MPG Books Ltd, Bodmin, Cornwall

Contents

List of illustrations   7

Acknowledgements   9

Abbreviations   10

1   A guide to the censuses of Ireland, 1813–1911   11

2   A place in time: territorial units in the censuses of Ireland   34

3   Census themes: tinkering and tailoring   44

4   Foraging and finding: the census as a research tool   81

Appendices   87
    I   Baronies of Ireland   87
    II   Counties of Ireland: notes   98
    III   Poor law unions of Ireland, 1841–51   99
    IV   Poor law unions and their county affiliations in 1851   100
    V   Adjustments to county affiliations of poor law unions between
       the 1851 and 1911 censuses   105
    VI   County electoral divisions of Ireland, 1901 and 1911   108
    VII   Urban and rural districts, 1901 and 1911   116

Census survey   127

Bibliography   149

Illustrations

FIGURES

1	Thomas Larcom, census commissioner, 1841	17
2	William Wilde, assistant census commissioner, 1851	18
3	Example of enumerator's form – 1st table, 2nd table and 3rd table	21
4	Thomas Wrigley Grimshaw, registrar-general, 1879–1900	31
5	Diagram showing the number of houses in each class, 1891 census	50
6	Report upon the table of deaths	74–5

TABLES AND DIAGRAM

1:1	Outline of column headings of Form A, 1st table, showing 'Return of Members, Visitors, and Servants of [the] Family', – Census of Ireland, 1851	23
2:1	Numbers of territorial units in Irish censuses, 1841–1911	42
3:1	Presentation of population statistics as printed in the *General Report* of the 1841 census	45
3:2	Population statistics as printed in the 1851 census: (a) parishes & townlands; (b) electoral divisions	46
3:3	Population statistics as printed in the 1871 census: (a) baronies; (b) poor law unions, registrars' districts & electoral divisions; (c) baronies, parishes and townlands	47
3:4	Spatial levels at which population statistics were enumerated, 1821–1911	48
3:5	Occupations of persons in the barony of Rosclogher, County Leitrim, 1821	51
3:6	Sample of occupations from the County Westmeath table, 1831	52
3:7	Table of occupations as presented in the 1831 census at parish and barony levels	53
3:8	Sample from the table of occupations as presented in the 1841 census for the parish, Killurin, in the barony of Shelmaliere, County Wexford	55
3:9	Sample of occupations from the County Mayo table, 1841	54
3:10	Sample of occupations for the province of Leinster by county in 1861	58
3:11	Table presentation of occupations in the 1901 & 1911 censuses at country level	60

3:12   Table showing the number and ages of literate and illiterate
           males in County Carlow, 1841   63
3:13(a)   Literacy levels of males showing numbers and ages in
           County Clare, 1851   64
3:13(b)   Female literacy as a percentage of female population in 1841 and
           1851 for County Clare, using the age cohorts of the 1841 census 65
3:14   Number and age of pupils attending school during the week
           ending 12 April 1851 in County Clare   65
3:15   Spatial levels at which literacy was enumerated   66
3:16   Literacy levels by age cohorts   67
3:17   Spatial levels at which language was enumerated   68
3:18   Age cohorts used in language tables of censuses, 1851–1911   68
3:19   Age bands of conjugal tables, 1841–1911   71
3:20   Presentation of morbidity statistics in censuses from 1881
           (on the census day)   72
3:21   Samples from the table of 'Cosmical Phenomena, Epizootics,
           Famines, and Pestilences, in Ireland'   76
3:22 (a)   A sample from County Carlow of 'Table I – Returns of
           Deaths, by Diseases, Sexes, Localities, and Years from 6th of June,
           1841, to 30th of March, 1851'   78
3:22 (b)   A sample from County Carlow of 'Table II – Returns of Deaths
           by Diseases, Sexes, and Ages from 6th of June, 1841,
           to 30th of March, 1851'   78
3:22 (c)   A sample from County Carlow of 'Table III – Returns of
in 2   Deaths, by Diseases and Seasons, in Localities from 6th of June,
parts   1841, to 30th of March, 1851'   79

Diagram 2:1   Principal administrative territorial units used in the
              Irish censuses   43

Acknowledgements

Much of the knowledge acquired to write this short book was gleaned while preparing selected statistics from the censuses of Ireland to form part of a large database of Irish Historical Statistics, funded by the ESRC. Co-operation of the librarians at the Queen's University of Belfast ensured access to these wonderful volumes thus easing the task, and so to them my grateful thanks. I would also like to thank Dr Patrick Duffy, Dr Raymond Gillespie for proposing this subject, and Dr Mary Ann Lyons, the editor of the series.

Abbreviations

BCB	Belfast county borough
CB	County boroughs
DC	Dublin city
DED	District electoral divisions
DS	Dublin suburbs
DMP	Dublin Metropolitan Police
DR	Dublin registration districts
HC	House of Commons
PLU	Poor law unions
RIC	Royal Irish Constabulary
RC	Registration counties
RP	Registration provinces

CHAPTER I

A guide to the censuses of Ireland, 1813–1911

INTRODUCTION

Census-taking has been the preserve of emperors, monarchs and rulers for centuries. Counting the people measured power, revenue and military might. From earliest times census enumeration has been unpopular with the populace who suspected it to be the fore-runner of conscription or increased taxation or some other unpleasant fate.

Fynes Moryson, an English visitor to Ireland at the beginning of the seventeenth century, guessed the population to be around 700,000 souls.[1] Sir William Petty made three estimates for the years 1672, 1676 and 1687, all based on the hearth-money returns (a tax on houses).[2] He was followed between the late seventeenth and early nineteenth centuries by Captain South, Arthur Dobbs, Gervaise Bushe, Daniel Beaufort and Thomas Newenham. In 1950 Professor K.H. Connell listed thirty estimates of population from 1672 to 1804, fourteen of which used the number of houses in Ireland, as returned by the hearth-money returns, to calculate the size of the population.[3] Arthur Young, a commentator on Irish agriculture, writing in 1780, urged the Irish legislature 'to order an actual enumeration of the whole people',[4] but this did not happen during the lifetime of the Irish parliament. Coherent attempts to estimate the population of Ireland have been discussed in detail by Brian Gurrin in a companion volume to this.[5]

In order to conduct a census an act of parliament was required. The Irish censuses of the period were taken under acts of the Westminster parliament – acts distinct from those setting up the censuses for Great Britain. The first official census of the population of Great Britain was taken in 1801. The relevant census act covered only England, Scotland and Wales, as it was passed in 1800 just before

1 See Herbert Woods, 'Estimating the population of Ireland before 1864', *Journal of the Statistical and Social Inquiry of Ireland*, xii (1909), p. 224.   2 William Petty also made a guess for 1641 of 1,466,000 people, and for 1652 of about 850,000.   3 K.H. Connell, *The population of Ireland, 1750 to 1845* (Oxford, 1950), pp 4–5.   4 Arthur Young, *A tour in Ireland: with general observations on the present state of that kingdom. Made in the years 1776, 1777, and 1778* (2 vols. 2nd ed. London, 1780), ii, p. 200.   5 Brian Gurrin, *Pre-census sources for Irish demography* (Dublin, 2002).

Ireland became part of the United Kingdom.[6] The Westminster government intended that there should be a census taken in Ireland, and in 1806 a bill was presented to parliament, but it failed to pass beyond the first reading.[7] A second census was taken of Great Britain in 1811, but Ireland again was excluded, because 'of the formidable practical difficulties'.[8] Finally, in 1812 the first Act for 'taking an account of the population of Ireland, and of the increase or diminution thereof', was passed.[9] Counting commenced in the following year. Despite a prolonged enumeration period, this census was never finished.

A completed census was achieved in 1821, and thereafter decennial censuses were conducted until 1911, when the last census of the entire island was taken by the British administration. Partition in 1921 interrupted the pattern. For all the Irish censuses up to 1911 there was separate legislation, even though the exercise was carried out in the same year as in Great Britain.

From uncertain beginnings the Irish censuses developed by the mid-nineteenth century into monumental works unrivalled elsewhere in the British Isles. Most of the enumerators' books[10] have been lost. Nevertheless, the published census reports are a rich source for our understanding of the economy and society in the period. This short book, focussing primarily on the ten published censuses from 1821 to 1911, is designed to guide the researcher into some of the fine minutiae of these works. It surveys the development in the design of the censuses, discusses the various territorial units used in the organization of statistics, examines a variety of topics covered in the censuses and, finally, reviews some of the more recent historical studies which drew on census data to develop a theme.

CENSUS OF IRELAND, 1813–15

William Shaw Mason was appointed to conduct the 1813–15 census. He was a government official with experience in organizing and collating social surveys,[11] having published a three-volume work entitled, *A statistical account, or parochial survey of Ireland* between 1814 and 1819.[12] He used the British census of 1811 as a model for administering the practical aspects of the exercise, but after two years the task was incomplete. Of the 32 counties and 8 cities and towns, only 10

6 The Act of Union came into operation on 1 January 1801.   7 *House of Commons Journal*, lxi, 14 Apr. 1806.   8 P. Froggatt, 'The census in Ireland of 1813–15', *Irish Historical Studies*, xiv, no. 55 (1965), p. 227.   9 52 Geo. III, c. 133.   10 Enumerator books contained the records of census details filled in either by the enumerator or the householder. 11 William Shaw Mason was simultaneously secretary to the record commission, joint-remembrancer of first fruits and comptroller of legacy duty in the stamp office. For more information see R.B. McDowell, *The Irish administration, 1801–1914* (London, 1964), pp 8–10.   12 W.S. Mason, *A statistical account or parochial survey of Ireland, drawn up from*

furnished complete returns; 24 submitted incomplete or inaccurate records and 6 counties made no returns. In the published census no population figures were recorded for the counties of Louth, Westmeath, Wexford, Cavan, Donegal and Sligo and the cities of Kilkenny and Limerick.

The failure was the consequence of poor local administration and the hostility of the Catholic population. Enumeration had been placed in the hands of the county grand juries, a body of men recruited from the ranks of landowners, agents, sons of the gentry and other Protestant members of the community. It was assumed that these juries would be the best suited for the task, but many lacked either the will or the organizational ability. In England poor law administrators were successfully deployed for this task, but in Ireland such personnel did not exist in 1813. The choice of grand jurors proved a poor substitute. Mason later reflected that they were 'not the best adapted to superintend the operations of a measure, requiring much time, much complex arrangement, and considerable minute responsibility in its execution'.[13]

The census information was gathered by verbal questioning. Barony constables and parish officers were recruited by grand juries to go from house to house seeking the numbers of people, though not their names, in the household. Constables were a poorly paid, part-time police force appointed by grand juries, who were not highly motivated to undertake this exacting and time consuming task. Furthermore they were Protestants, not the most suitable qualification for enumerating a largely mistrusting Catholic population. Finally, there was no procedure to monitor the accuracy of their work. In the event, the returns received were deemed unreliable and so unsuitable for presentation to parliament. Mason was unsparing in his criticism of the constables, describing them as 'inferior agents' who were guilty of 'deficiency of information in some instances, and want of zeal on other'.[14] Nevertheless by a combination of the partial results and some creative accounting, a population count of 5,937,856 was finally published for 1813.[15]

CENSUS OF IRELAND FOR THE YEAR 1821

The census of 1821 commenced on 28 May with William Shaw Mason again at the helm. Learning from the unsatisfactory experience of 1813–15, he drew up different enumeration procedures with the aim of achieving a higher level of accuracy. The supervision of data collection 'was transferred from the Grand Juries to the Bench of Magistrates ... aided by the advice of a permanent legal Coadjutor'.[16] Tax collectors were usually employed as enumerators. To test the ability of the enumerators, preliminary returns had to be submitted before the candidate was accepted for the real exercise. At this point some resigned, realizing the task was beyond their ability, while others were found unfit for the job. In an effort to overcome the population's hostility, contact was made with local clergymen, who were asked to assist in 'controlling the proceedings of the Enumerators …, and for removing any prejudices, … that might tend to produce an unkindly feeling towards them in the minds of the lower classes.'[17]

An initial obstacle to the collection of information was the lack of maps defining spatial boundaries and incomplete lists of parish and townland names. Thus, 'when the Irish census officials conceived the notion of calculating local population densities they found that the areas of many townlands and parishes were still unknown, let alone measured'.[18] Up to the 1830s Ireland had been mapped in a piecemeal fashion, though this was in the process of being remedied with the creation of the Irish Ordnance Survey department in 1824. Between 1833 and 1846 a townland survey of the entire country with six-inch maps was undertaken, but these were too late for either the 1821 or 1831 censuses. In fact, townlands caused 'much embarrassment in the progress of the Census'[19] because in some areas no record of a territorial unit smaller than a parish existed. Hence as part of the census exercise, the enumerators were required to state the number of acres in each townland in their area. To aid in establishing a spatial framework for the collection and recording of censal information, the returns submitted to the Chief Secretary's Office in Dublin contained a census of 'every distinct or subordinate division of Land in Ireland', organized in the following manner:

1. The Name and Situation of every Townland, subdivision of Townland, or other smallest territorial district, … classed according to its Parish, Barony and County;
2. The Name of every Town, Village and Hamlet, in each County, with, … the number of houses in each;
3. The Name and Situation of every Street, Square, Lane, Alley, Court … in Cities and Corporate Towns;
4. The Number of Dwelling Houses …, whether inhabited, uninhabited or building …;
5. The Number, names and situation, of all public Buildings …[20]

The information sought from householders and recorded in the returns was as follows:

1. Name age and occupation of every person resident in Ireland;
2. Number of families and relationships within the family units;

---

17 Ibid., p. xii.   18 J.H. Andrews, *A paper landscape: the Ordnance Survey in nineteenth-century Ireland* (Oxford, 1975; repr. Dublin, 2002), p. 14.   19 *Census of Ireland*, 1821, p. x.   20 Ibid., p. xiii.

3. Quantity of land held by each person in the townland in which resident;
4. Number of schools with the number of pupils in attendance.

The published abstract presented to parliament was prepared for parishes, towns, and villages aggregated up to barony, county and provincial levels. Counties and baronies were an obvious choice as they were already in use for fiscal and administrative purposes. While baronies fitted neatly into counties[21] the same was not true of parishes. They crossed boundaries, and civil and ecclesiastical parish boundaries did not always correspond either.

The 1821 census was a great improvement on its predecessor. It was completed, had an abstract prepared, and was published. The abstract contained population statistics, a survey of housing stock with the number of families in inhabited houses, employment statistics of main occupational groups, a pupil census and an age profile of the population. However, over a three-year period three population estimates were published, indicating some uncertainty about accuracy. The first estimate, in November 1821, stated that Ireland's population numbered 6,648,033.[22] A second figure, 6,846,949, appeared in the *Abstract of the Population of Ireland according to the late census* printed in 1822. Two years later the *Abstract of Answers and Returns under the Population Act of Ireland, 1821* published a figure of 6,801,826. Subsequent scrutiny suggests a degree of underenumeration. Thomas Larcom, a commissioner on the 1841 census, believed the census figure to be 'rather below than above the truth'. One reason was the uneven quality of enumerators' work notwithstanding preliminary testing. The transfer of responsibility for enumeration from grand juries to resident magistrates made little or no difference since magistrates and grand jurors were often the same people.[23] The second reason for concern was the suspicion of the population towards the enumerators, despite clerical intercession. More recently, J.J. Lee has examined the census and suggested a 5 per cent underestimation, producing a figure of 7.2 million.[24]

CENSUS OF IRELAND FOR THE YEAR 1831

A new commissioner, George Hatchell, organized the 1831 census. He was a government official who subsequently had a key role in the establishment of a Public Records Office for Ireland. The enumeration was organized on similar lines to the 1821 census. For instance, enumerators travelled from house to house

21 In a few cases there were small 'tongues' of land which dipped over into adjoining counties. **22** Shaw Mason Papers, TCD MSS 1734, cited in J.J. Lee, 'On the accuracy of the pre-Famine Irish censuses' in J.M. Goldstrom & L.A. Clarkson (eds), *Irish population, economy and society: essays in honour of the late K.H. Connell*, in (Oxford, 1981), p. 44. **23** J.J. Lee, 'On the accuracy', p. 39. **24** Ibid., p. 46.

verbally requesting the relevant information, though unlike the 1821 census, names of all the inhabitants were not required, only those of the household heads. This was the last census which used the *viva voce* method to collect the household details.

The 1831 census has been subjected to much criticism. Firstly, 'it was taken in different places at different times, extending over a considerable period'.[25] This procedure, though, was not new. Secondly, the process of collecting the information by vocal inquiry was also criticized, yet it was used before. Thirdly, 'enumerators considered that they would be paid – and in many cases were paid – in proportion to the numbers they enumerated', leading to the temptation of over-counting.[26] However, as Lee has pointed out, 'there was nothing unique about the specified payment procedures in 1831';[27] they were the same as those used in 1821. Remuneration was generally levied by the day and not per person enumerated. In practice some enumerators were paid per head recorded, thus giving rise to allegations of over-enumeration. Like the previous census, Lee believes the 7,767,401 souls returned in 1831 to be an underestimation. A more realistic figure he estimates would be 7.9 million.[28] Finally, the published census lacked an introduction, leaving us in the dark about its planning and execution. The omission has been interpreted as an admission of inadequacy, though Lee suggests it may have been due more to an alertness on the part of George Hatchell 'to the inherent problems of census-taking in Ireland', than any, 'implicit confession of inadequacy'.[29] Moreover, statistics on the age structure of the population and pupil numbers were not recorded.

THE CENSUS OF IRELAND FOR THE YEAR 1841

The 1841 census was a milestone in census-taking. It inaugurated fundamental changes that established the process for subsequent census enumeration. It broke new ground in the range of information collected and in the presentation of results. A gauge of the esteem this work is held can be found in the *General Report* to the first census of the Irish Free State in 1926, where the writer commented; 'the remarkable Census of 1841 merits particular attention even these days, not only because many of the features introduced at this enumeration have been used at all subsequent Censuses, but also because of its intrinsic excellence.'[30]

Three commissioners were appointed – William Tighe Hamilton, Henry J. Brownrigg, and Thomas Larcom. Hamilton was a young lawyer from the Chief Secretary's Office; Brownrigg, a former army officer and an inspector in the

25 *Report of the Commissioners appointed to take the census of Ireland for the year 1841* (hereafter *Census Report, 1841*), H.C. 1843 (504), xxiv, p. viii.   26 *Census Report, 1841*, p. viii.   27 Lee, 'On the accuracy', p. 47.   28 Ibid., p. 53.   29 Ibid., p. 52.   30 *Saorstát Éireann, Census of Population, 1926, x, General Report* (Dublin, 1934), p. 3.

1 Thomas Larcom, census commissioner, 1841

Royal Irish Constabulary; and Larcom was recruited from the Ordnance Survey Office. There was one other notable person in the team, William Wilde. He was an eminent aural and ophthalmic surgeon, who was appointed as a contracted assistant. Wilde was an interesting addition to the census commission. He had 'statistical interest, experience of Irish folk habits, language, and *mores*, literacy ability and professional and historical flair',[31] all highly valuable skills for the analysis of the census data. He approached this work with great zeal and 'threw himself into the task with his customary energy, compiling vast numbers of tables, adding, subtracting, analysing and record and doing a great quantity of what another would have thought unnecessary work.'[32]

Larcom was the architect of this census. He was well qualified to undertake the task, having gained a wealth of experience in social inquiry while working in the Ordnance Survey Office. An army engineer by profession, Larcom trained as a surveyor, and in addition to mapping the country, he included the collection of material for local surveys. A 37-page pamphlet, designed by Larcom, outlined the framework for a statistical, geological, antiquarian, social and topographical

31 P. Froggatt, 'Sir William Wilde, 1815–1876', *Proceedings of the Royal Irish Academy*, lxxvii, C, no. 10 (1977), p. 264. 32 T.G. Wilson, *Victorian doctor: life of Sir William Wilde* (London, 1942), p. 131.

2 William Wilde, assistant census commissioner, 1851

survey referred to as a *memoir*. Unfortunately, the *memoirs* were never completed because of lack of money.[33] This task gave Larcom new ideas for designing and presenting the census.

33 T.A. Larcom, *Ordnance Survey of the County Londonderry. Memoir of the city and north western liberties of Londonderry. Parish of Templemore* (Dublin, 1837), was the only memoir

There were several changes in the planning and execution of this census. Members of the recently formed Royal Irish Constabulary and the Dublin Metropolitan Police force, supplemented by other central government officers, formed the team of enumerators. The co-operation and assistance of the Constabulary explained Brownrigg's inclusion on the commission. The former practice of using constables appointed by grand juries and tax collectors as enumerators was discontinued, greater confidence being placed in the new police force, who were used for subsequent censuses and for the collection of annual agricultural statistics that commenced in 1847.

Two forms (A and B) were used for collecting the census information. 'Form A' was distributed to each household prior to census day for the head of the household to fill in. This method was viewed 'as less intrusive than ... from *viva voce* inquiry'[34] of the previous censuses. At the point of collection the return was checked and the enumerator had to certify that the information was 'true to the best of his belief.'[35] Where householders failed to fill in the form, enumerators were empowered to elicit the relevant information and complete the task.

'Form A' contained three tables. On the first table was returned 'the Members, Servants, and Visitors of this Family, *who slept in this house* on the night of Sunday, the 6 June, 1841.'[36] Details of names, age, sex, relationship to head of family, conjugal status, year of marriage, occupation of those family members working, level of literacy and place of origin were requested. The second table was designed to collect the same information about household members who were absent on the night of 6 June 1841. Conjugal status and literacy levels were not requested, though there was a question asking where these absent people were residing on the census date. The third table recorded those family members who had died while residing in the household since the previous census on 6 June 1831. Name, age, sex, relation to household head, occupations, cause of death and the year of demise were requested. An additional section at the bottom of Table 1, posed three questions about agricultural employment. The first inquired as to how many people were usually employed on farms daily. The second question asked for the total number of days worked by men and women. The final question requested details of wages paid to men and women, excluding diet as a component of the remuneration. Unfortunately the answers were not published.

The enumerator completed 'Form B'. It recorded information about property and the numbers of families living in each abode. The enumerator had to evaluate the quality of every house in his area, and place it into one of four categories, using guidelines issued by the census office. Statistics were also

published at the time. More recently Ordnance Surveys Memoirs for the northern half of the country have been edited and published in 40 volumes by Angélique Day and Patrick McWilliams, The Institute for Irish Studies, The Queen's University of Belfast. See also Thomas E. Jordan, *An imaginative empiricist: Thomas Aiskew Larcom, 1801–1879 and Victorian Ireland* (Lampeter, 2002). **34** *Census Report, 1841*, p. v. **35** Ibid., **36** Ibid., p. xci. Note that

collected on farm size, how the land was utilized and the number and type of livestock. Finally, the number of separate families living in each house along with the names of every family head had to be recorded. This housing survey was a unique feature of the Irish census.

The final result was a census of two volumes: the *Report* published in 1843,[37] and the *Addenda*,[38] issued the next year. The *Report* featured a vast array of social and economic statistics. This census was a work of greater breadth and vision than its predecessors. It included for the first time statistics of births, deaths and marriages, important in the absence of compulsory registration, and introduced tables of literacy levels and data on the rural economy. Larcom achieved his aim of producing 'a social survey, not bare enumeration'.[39] The *Addenda* contained the more conventional enumeration of people, houses and families, published for the first time at townland level.

Wilde's contribution was impressive too. For his *Report upon the Table of Deaths* he composed a commentary of 74 closely printed pages, prepared 205 tables and compiled a nosology,[40] grouping diseases into classes with popular and local names in both English and Irish. He laid the foundations in 1841 for comparative analysis of vital statistics between England and Ireland in anticipation of compulsory registration of births, marriages and deaths. His preparation included adopting, with small variations, the classification of diseases:

> used … in the Reports of the Registrar-General of Births, Deaths, and Marriages in England, not only because it appear[ed] … the simplest and yet most scientific, but in order that comparisons may … be made between the diseases and mortality of the two countries.[41]

Wilde's tables and report on deaths were highly acclaimed. The editor of the *Dublin Journal of Medical Science*, reviewing his contribution to the 1841 census, acknowledged that it did 'him [Wilde] infinite credit, both as to the mode adopted for obtaining accurate results, and the labour and extreme care bestowed'.[42]

THE CENSUS OF IRELAND FOR THE YEAR 1851

Further changes to the organization were introduced in 1851. The Registrar-General's Office undertook the census for the first time,[43] and from there all

the word 'family' was used to define the inhabitants of the entire household. It was not confined to kinship members only.   **37** Ibid.   **38** *Addenda to the census of Ireland for the years 1841* (Dublin, 1844).   **39** McDowell, *The Irish administration*, p. 283.   **40** Nosology is the term used to describe the science of disease classification.   **41** *Census Report, 1841*, 'Report upon the table of deaths', Section 1, p. v. In the event compulsory registration in Ireland was not in place by the next census or even the following one.   **42** Cited in P. Froggatt, 'The demographic work of Sir William Wilde', *Irish Journal of Medical Science*, vi (1965), p. 214.   **43** In 1844 a Registrar-General's Office was established for Ireland

1ST TABLE.—Return of the Members, Servants, and Visitors of this Family, *who slept in this house* on the night of Sunday, the 6th June, 1841.

Christian Names.	Surnames.	Years.	Months.	Whether Male or Female.	RELATION Of each to the Head of family, as whether Wife, Son, Daughter, Cousin, Servant, Visitor, &c.	Whether "Married," "Not Married," "Widower," or "Widow."	In what year married, or in what years if more than once.	OCCUPATION. State the particular Profession, Trade, or other Employment; or if a child, whether attending School.	EDUCATION. Whether he or she can "Read," "Read and Write," or "Cannot Read."	Native of what Country, County, or City.
John .	Moran, .	59	–	Male,	Head of Family,	Married,	1805	Farmer, . .	Read, . .	Kildare.
Eliza .	Moran, .	55	–	Female,	Wife, . .	Married, .	1805	. . . .	Cannot Read, .	Do.
George	Moran, .	28	–	Male,	Son, . .	Not Married,	–	Woollen Weaver, .	Read and Write,	Do.
Matilda	Moran, .	23	–	Female,	Daughter, .	Not Married,	–	Spinning Wool, .	Do. . .	Do.
Jane .	Moran, .	16	–	Female,	Daughter, .	Not Married,	–	Do. . .	Do. . .	Do.
John .	Moran, .	13	–	Male,	Son, . .	Not Married,	–	At Mr. Daly's school,	Do. . .	Do.
Mary .	Mathers, .	45	–	Female,	Sister-in-Law,	Not Married,	–	None, . .	Do. . .	Do.
Peter .	Macdonald, .	24	–	Male,	Servant, . .	Married,	1836	Labourer, . .	Do. . .	Scotland.
Peggy	Butler, .	22	–	Female,	Do. . .	Not Married,	–	House Servant, .	Cannot Read, .	Dublin.
Jane .	Whitmore, .	23	–	Female,	Visitor, . .	Not Married,	–	None, . . .	Read and Write,	England.

Question :—What Number of Persons usually resort to the FARM for daily Employment ?
Answer : {Males, No. of 5 | [a] Total Number of days' Work given to Males in one year, 150 | Wages of Males per day without diet, 10*d*.
{Females, do. 2 | Ditto, ditto, to Females in do. 100 | Wages of Females per day without diet, 4*d*

[a] It is to be observed the number of Days' Work will be ascertained by multiplying the number of persons employed by the number of days they work, thus, in the example given above, 5 men have worked 30 days each, and 2 females 50 days each.

2ND TABLE.—Return of Members of this Family now alive, and *whose home is* in this House, but *who were absent* on the night of Sunday, the 6th June, 1841.

Christian Names.	Surnames.	Years.	Months.	Whether Male or Female.	RELATION Of each to the Head of the Family, whether Wife, Son, Daughter, Cousin, Servant, Visitor, &c.	OCCUPATION. State the particular Profession, Trade, or other Employment; or if a Child, whether attending School.	In what Country, County, or City, at present Residing.
Timothy .	Moran, .	31	–	Male,	Son, . .	Army, . .	America.
Eliza .	Moran, .	26	–	Female,	Daughter, . .	None, . .	Dublin.
William .	Moran, .	18	–	Male,	Son, . .	Haymaker . .	England.
Thomas .	Moran, .	22	–	Male,	Son, . .	Constabulary, .	County Down.

3RD TABLE.—Return of Members of this Family, Servants, or Visitors, who have *died while residing with this Family*, since the 6th June, 1831.—Thirty-one.

Christian Names.	Surnames.	Years.	Mon.	Whether Male or Female.	RELATION Of each to the Head of the Family, whether Wife, Son, Daughter, Cousin, Servant, Visitor, &c.	OCCUPATION. State the particular Profession, Trade, or other Employment.	Disease which caused Death.	In what year died.
William .	Moran, .	80	–	Male, .	Father, . .	Farmer, . .	Apoplexy .	1832
Alexander .	Moran, .	10	–	Male, .	Son, . .	None, . .	Small Pox,	1840

Signature of Person making and affirming Return. }

Affirmed by the foregoing, before me, the   day of   1841.
In conformity with Act 3 & 4 VICT., cap. 100.

_____Magistrate.

M 2

3 Example of enumerator's form – 1st table, 2nd table and 3rd table

subsequent censuses up to and including that of 1911 were organized. The officers in charge of the project were William Donnelly, the registrar-general, also appointed as the census commissioner, and William Wilde, as the assistant census commissioner. Wilde's highly acclaimed work for the 1841 census 'whetted [his] appetite for statistical enquiry, and from that time on he was determined to play a major role in the census of 1851.'[44] Edward Singleton was added to the team as secretary. Thomas Larcom was indisposed and unable to serve. As with the 1841 census the enumerators were selected from the Constabulary and DMP force who were supplemented by 'other competent persons'.

Census day was 30 March 1851, and the process of collecting information from households remained the same as that of the 1841 census. However, in scale there was no comparison. This census was the most comprehensive so far, and included several unique features. Indeed it was unrivalled by censuses in any other country.[45] Thirteen forms were designed for the collection of information, listed as follows.

Form A   household return (3 tables)
Form B   housing and family return along with the ship return (2 tables)
Form C   return of those who were ill on the night of the census (1 table)
Form D   return of the insane and idiots (1 table)
Form E   return of paupers in workhouses – able-bodied, sick & deceased (3 tables)
Form F   return of the sick in hospitals and those who had died in hospital from 6 June 1841 to 30 March 1851 (2 tables)
Form G   return of teachers and students resident in colleges (1 table)
Form H   return of military personnel (1 table)
Form I   return of persons treated in public lunatic asylums (2 tables)
Form K   return of prisoners (1 table)
Form L   return of scholars attending school during week ending 19 April 1851 (1 table)
Form O   return of emigrants and passengers (1 table)
Form P   returns of inquests from 6 June 1841 to 30 March 1851 (1 table)

As in 1841 'Form A' contained three tables. The first requested information about family members, visitors and servants, shown in *Table 1.1*. An additional feature was statistics about the deaf, the dumb and the blind Sensitivity surrounding these disabilities was appreciated prompting some debate about how this information could best be collected.[46] Once a disabled individual had

because an amendment to the Irish marriage law required the recording of all non-Catholic marriages from 1845.   **44** P. Froggatt, 'Sir William Wilde and the 1851 census', *Medical History*, ix (1965), p. 305.   **45** Ibid., p. 302.   **46** Information on the deaf, dumb

Table 1:1. Outline of column headings of 'Form A', 1st Table,
showing 'Return of the Members, Visitors, and Servants of
[the] Family', – Census of Ireland, 1851

Names	Age	Sex	Relation	Marriage	Rank, profession or occupation	Education	Where born	Whether deaf-and-dumb, or blind

been identified, the household was visited by an enumerator, usually a local policeman, who carried out a supplementary enquiry.[47] The second table of 'Form A' was for the enumeration of absent family members on the enumeration night. On the third table, mortality statistics were collected. As in 1841, 'Form A' was distributed in advance of the census date for heads of households to complete on census day. Collection was to begin on Monday 31 March 1851.

As before, the enumerator filled in 'Form B'. The form was in two sections. One was for the collection of details about houses, such as materials used for constructing the building, its function, the number of stories, rooms and windows. The second section was for the enumeration of discrete family groups living within each abode. Two columns (male and female) were also included for recording the number of people in the family who were sick on census day. The guidelines provided in 1841 to aid in this task were used again in 1851. The second section was for a return of shipping including ships, boats, vessels, yachts, fishing and other boats in ports, harbours, bays, canals, lakes and rivers. Crews and passengers were also recorded along with their nationality. The recording of cereal yields and animal numbers ceased because a more elaborate scheme for the gathering of annual agricultural statistics was introduced by the Registrar-General's Office in 1847. Nevertheless, although the 1851 agricultural statistics were not collected as part of the census enumeration exercise, they were 'added to those of the general Census, in conformity with his Excellency's desire.'[48]

Disease was another new theme. Morbidity statistics were collected, collated and published in a report dedicated to disease. The data were divided into nine categories:

    (i)   deaf and dumb
    (ii) blind

and blind was also requested on forms A, E, F, I and L (i.e.) from Masters of workhouses, superintendents of hospitals, keepers of asylums, gaols and school principals.   **47** For contents of the special questionnaire on the deaf, dumb and blind see *Census of Ireland for the year 1851*, part vi, *General Report*, H.C. 1856 [2134], xxxi, p. cxxxvi.   **48** *An Act for the taking an account of the population of Ireland*, 13 & 14 Vict., c. 44. *The Census of Ireland for the*

(iii) lunatics and idiots

(iv) lame and decrepit

(v) inmates in workhouses

(vi) sick in hospitals

(vii) sick in asylums

(viii) the inmates in prisons

(ix) total sick in Ireland

The local knowledge of the enumerators qualified them to fill in this form with accuracy, although 'where Lunatics or Idiots [were] in the custody of their friends, [there was an appreciation that] the inquiries necessary … should be made with *the greatest delicacy*.'[49] 'Form E' enumerated pauper sicknesses in the workhouse hospitals, and the sick in general hospitals and public lunatic asylums were recorded in 'Form F' and 'Form I' respectively.

There was a growing awareness of the importance of medical statistics, and William Wilde was at the forefront of this area of study. The gathering of information on disease and death was exclusively his work. These data were published in three volumes, one on disease, and two on deaths. In addition to an analysis of mortality statistics, the first volume of deaths included a table of the 'history of epidemic pestilences in Ireland' and a catalogue of 'cosmical phenomena, epizootics, epiphitics, famines and pestilences in Ireland'. Although not unique, this work has been described as 'a classic of great scholarship, erudition and industry'.[50] Ireland still lacked civil registration of death, and in his report on disease Wilde's exasperation at this deficiency spilled over, as he commented that the insertion of nosological classification was 'a useful prelude to the introduction of any general registration of deaths, so universally called for in Ireland'.[51]

The gathering of information to measure educational attainment was maintained and developed. In addition to seeking data on the literacy level of the population, information was sought to identify those who spoke both Irish and English and those who spoke only Irish. Statistics on both literacy and language were collected for subsequent censuses until 1911. Returns were made of the number of scholars attending schools during a particular week, together with the age and sex of the pupils, the occupation of their parents, and if the tuition was free or had to be paid for. Also included on the educational enumeration form was a list of subjects taught to students.[52]

To summarize, 1851 was a huge census of ten volumes, and was one of the greatest national censuses of the nineteenth century.[53] Four volumes, one for

years 1851, part ii, *Returns of agricultural produce in 1851*, H.C. 1852–3 [1589], xciii, p. i. **49** *The Census of Ireland for the years 1851*, part vi, *General Report*, p. cxxx.   **50** Froggatt, 'Sir William Wilde and the 1851 Census', p. 306.   **51** *The Census of Ireland for the year 1851*, part iii, *Report upon the status of disease*, H.C. 1854 [1765], lviii, p. 113.   **52** See *The Census of Ireland for the year 1851*, part iv. *Report on ages and education*, H.C. 1856 [2053], xxix, p. lvi.   **53** Froggatt, 'The demographic work of Sir William Wilde', p. 216.

each province, contained the enumeration of population and housing stock at townland and electoral division level. Figures were also included for 1841 to facilitate comparison. A fifth volume presented returns of agricultural production. Three more volumes were devoted to disease and deaths, another recorded statistics on education and age profile of the population. A final volume contained the *General Report*.

THE CENSUS OF IRELAND FOR THE YEAR 1861

Once again Donnelly and Wilde were appointed as commissioner and assistant commissioner for the 1861 census. Another physician, Dr George Whitley Abraham, was added to the team as a second assistant commissioner. During the intervening decade Larcom had been appointed to the post of under secretary in 1853 and Brownrigg promoted to head of the Royal Irish Constabulary in 1858. Census day was 7 April 1861, and collection of the forms commenced the following day with the expectation that the task would be completed within ten days. This time-scale proved over ambitious. Nevertheless, an abstract census was presented to the houses of parliament on 12 July 1861 containing statistics on provinces, counties, boroughs, cities and towns.

The census machinery was now well oiled; only minor adjustments were required. Once again the RIC and DMP were used for the enumeration process: additional civilian personnel were no longer necessary. There were twelve enumeration forms, and all followed a similar pattern to those of 1851, with a few design changes. One change was the omission of 'Form O', formerly used to record emigrants. The need to collect these statistics as part of the census became redundant, because in 1851 the government ordered that persons leaving Ireland permanently be recorded at ports of exit. These emigration statistics then appeared annually from 1857 until 1875 together with the agricultural returns. From 1871 to 1911 emigration figures compiled from returns supplied by the Registrar-General's Office were published for each county in the census.[54]

A major innovation in the 1861 census was the inclusion of information on religion. The Irish acts for both the 1841 and 1851 censuses directed that 'no Reference to the Religion of any person or persons' be taken.[55] The census acts for England and Wales, and Scotland up to and including the 1861 census did

54 For detailed explanation see W.E. Vaughan and A.J. Fitzpatrick (eds), *Irish historical statistics: population, 1821–1971* (Dublin, 1978), pp xvi–xvii. For emigration data from 1851 to 1911 by county see *Census of Ireland, 1911*, part i, vols i–iv, H.C. 1912–13 [Cd. 6049], cxiv; H.C. 1912–13 [Cd. 6050], cxv; H.C. 1912–13 [Cd. 6051], cxvi; H.C. 1912–13 [Cd. 6052], cxvii (Table XLI of each county). **55** 3 & 4 Vict. c.100, *An Act for taking an account of the population of Ireland*; 13 & 14 Vict. c. 44, *An Act for taking an account of the population of Ireland*.

not include the gathering of information on religion either. The 1861 Irish census was, therefore, an exception.[56]

A special report was prepared to accompany the section on religion.[57] It provided a brief history of early attempts to survey religious beliefs in Ireland. In *c*.1672 William Petty had estimated the numbers of Roman Catholics, Episcopalians and Non-conformists in Ireland.[58] Another attempt at a religious census was made in 1736 based on the hearth-money returns for the years 1732 and 1733.[59] This work was later criticized on the grounds that 'it neither attempts to distinguish between different denominations of Protestants, nor to give any idea, however imperfect, of the occupations and social position of Protestant and Roman Catholic'.[60] In 1834 a Royal Commission was appointed to 'Inquire into the State of Religious and other instruction in Ireland'.[61] The remit was wide and included the recording of a census of members in the different religious denominations, though it did not pass without criticism either. The authors of the 1861 census report were dissatisfied that only four religious denominations – Established Church, Roman Catholics, Presbyterians, and other Protestant Dissenters – were identified.

The 1861 commissioners decided on nine denominational headings – Established Church, Roman Catholics, Presbyterians, Methodists, Independents, Baptists, Society of Friends or Quakers, Jews, and 'Other Persuasions'. The last category included 112 identified sects recorded in a separate table. In addition to a religious census there was included an analysis of literacy levels, school attendance and occupations according to religious profession. The religious census was published in *Reports and Tables relating to the religious profession, education and occupations of the people* (two volumes),[62] and in the *General Report*.

The complete census was published in eleven volumes. Four volumes, one for each province, recorded the results of the household enumeration, two further volumes contained data on education and age, one volume (not two as in 1851) presented the deaths statistics, and another was devoted to disease. Data on religious profession were published in two volumes, and the final volume was the *General Report*.

---

56 As part of the 1851 census of England, Scotland and Wales an enumeration was taken of Church attendance – *Religious Worship (England and Wales) Report*, HC 1852–3 [1690], lxxxix and for Scotland, HC 1854 [1764], lix.   57 *The census of Ireland for the year 1861, part iv, Reports and tables relating to the religious profession, education and occupations of the people*, vols i & ii, H.C. 1863 [3204–III], lix & lx.   58 William Petty, *The political anatomy of Ireland* (London, 1691; repr. Shannon, 1970), p. 8.   59 *An abstract of the number of Protestants and Popish families in the several counties and provinces of Ireland taken from the returns made by the Hearth money collectors to the Hearth Money Office in the years 1732 and 1733, those being reckoned Protestant or popish families where the Heads of the Families are either Protestant or Popish* (Dublin, 1736).   60 *The Census of Ireland for the year 1861*, part iv, vol. i, p. 3.   61 *Commission for inquiring into the state of religious and other instruction in Ireland*, H.C. 1834 (356), xliii.   62 *The Census of Ireland for the year 1861*, part iv, *Reports ... religious*

THE CENSUS OF IRELAND FOR THE YEAR 1871

Messrs Donnelly, Wilde and Abraham formed the commission for yet another census, with Henry Wilkie as secretary. The second of April 1871 was selected as census day. The Irish commissioners were now well practised in the art of census-taking, and work had already started according to the pattern used in 1861. Instructions then arrived from the office of the Registrar-General in London to follow 'a series of pattern tables transmitted …, [which covered] the whole ground plan of the English Census.'[63] These changes were prompted by the Statistical Committee of the British Association, which was keen on uniformity throughout the entire kingdom. The Irish commissioners were not best pleased by this directive. For one thing, the statistical analysis for one county was already completed in the 'old style'. Secondly, the Irish commissioners were confident that their census presentation was superior to that of the Great Britain.

The ire of the Irish commissioners was apparent in several scathing comments published in the *General Report* to the 1871 census. They asserted that the decision to change the presentation of the Irish census was founded 'upon a very superficial reading of the Irish census publications; upon acquaintance next to none with the local circumstances imposing a necessary individuality on many of the Irish statistics'; and finally, 'a total omission of reference to the provisions of the Irish Census Acts'.[64] The commissioners assured Earl Spencer, the viceroy, 'that the idea of disputing [the new format] could never have occurred to us'. Yet they went on to argue that 'nothing could be less worthy of statistical science than condescension to the pedantries of a forced uniformity'.[65] This particular outburst was prompted by the 'invitation' from the London census office to group the Irish figures into 'Divisions of Lieutenancy', 'Local Board districts' and 'Hundreds', all territorial units that did not exist in Ireland.

The London office caused the Irish commissioners further irritation with its criticism of the presentation of occupational statistics in the previous Irish censuses. According to London, the Irish occupational statistics were not broken down according to age. This was simply not true, and a sharp response pointed to the presence of the alleged omission. Further acrimony occurred over the classification of occupations. The Irish commissioners were proud of their own scheme, alluding to

> a time, more than thirty years ago, when ideas upon this subject were crude and elementary, even among the best informed, [when] … a long stride forward was made by the Irish Census Commission of the day … [to produce a] scheme of Occupational Tables, according to which the

profession, education and occupations of the People, vols i & ii. **63** *Census of Ireland, 1871*, part iii, *General Report*, H.C. 1876 [C. 1377], lxxxi, p. 2. **64** Ibid., p. 2. **65** Ibid., p. 3.

ranks, pursuits, and means of subsistence of the Irish people have been presented in the Census returns of 1841, 1851, and 1861.[66]

They contended that 'we do not know that it has been surpassed or equalled in accuracy by any other scheme' and, 'it resembles, in all events, the Linnæan distribution of plants'.[67] The vitriolic comments continued, with the Irish commissioners highlighting certain aspects of the English occupational tables for sharp criticism. The art of occupational classification was still in its infancy, and the Irish commissioners were so confident of their methods that they did not take kindly to it being cast aside by the London census officials. In the end the English occupational classification had to be adopted, at least in the county tables. However, not content to abandon entirely the Irish classification, county, provincial and national tables were prepared according to the Irish scheme and published in the *General Report*. This was to be the last census to use this occupational classification.

The Irish commissioners were further aggrieved by the late arrival of the instructions. The returns for three counties had already been completed to the first stage using the old formula. Furthermore, the Irish commissioners were keen 'to keep in line with the general advance of statistical science' as well as maintain the high standard that in their view the Irish censuses had achieved. There was, nevertheless, a distinct benefit to the pattern used in the British census. The British format, referred to by the Irish office as the 'Imperial Census', organized the census statistics into single county volumes, which were individually bound and could be purchased as such. With the exception of detailed disease and mortality statistics, thematic volumes were now redundant, all other themes being presented in the county books.

The census of 1871 established the mould for successive censuses. In all, 34 separate county and county borough books, each containing 41 tables, were published along with a volume of Vital Statistics (Disease and Deaths) and a *General Report*. The statistics were grouped into the following ten themes:

1. Area, housing and population
2. Ages of the population
3. Civil or conjugal status
4. Occupations of the population
5. Birthplaces of the population
6. Statistics of resident foreigners in Ireland
7. Statistics of the blind, deaf and dumb, lunatics, paupers etc. and tables of deaths
8. Religious profession of the population
9. Religious profession and education of the population
10. Emigration statistics

66 Ibid., p. 64.   67 Ibid.

The 1871 census was the swan-song of specialized volumes on disease and deaths for two reasons. Firstly, annual reports of the Registrar-General now included the number and causes of deaths, making redundant the inclusion of this material in the census. Secondly, the 1871 census was the last William Wilde worked on,[68] and since morbidity and mortality statistics were his particular *forte*, interest in epidemiological data disappeared along with him. Wilde's dedication to the censuses 1841–71 was impressive, and his contribution was highly praised by contemporaries, culminating in his knighthood for services to the census in 1864. Although the recording of biological statistics was not unique to the Irish census, there was nothing quite like it in the British censuses. Some European countries enumerated the deaf and dumb, and some countries collected and analysed mortality returns, but the statistics and analyses presented in the Irish censuses produced a 'result constitut[ing] without doubt the most important and comprehensive population data on a physical handicap'. It was the scale and depth of Wilde's work which were remarkable and a worthy testimony to his talent for understanding the 'fundamentals of demographic enquiry'.[69]

Despite all the huffing and puffing, the Irish commissioners proudly announced that the Irish census was considerably more voluminous than either its English or Scottish counterparts, comprising 5,606 pages compared with 2,384 and 1,168 pages respectively. More subjects were featured in the Irish census and statistics were tabulated for 71,923 places in Ireland, compared with only 15,416 for England.

THE CENSUS OF IRELAND FOR THE YEAR 1881

By 1881 a new registrar-general, Thomas Wrigley Grimshaw, was in post. A distinguished Dublin doctor by profession, he was appointed in September 1879. Another newcomer was a lawyer, Robert E. Matheson. Dr Abraham was the only member of the 1871 commission to be also involved in the 1881 census, and having by now been promoted to a commissioner. Census day was 3 April 1881. The 1871 pattern for the county tables was used with a few small modifications.

A new feature of the census was a land survey. This innovation was in response to a suggestion of the Statistical and Social Inquiry Society of Ireland to collect information on the number of people living on farms of different sizes, and the numbers of migratory agricultural labourers employed for up to six weeks in the year outside the electoral division or union in which they lived.[70] In the event the number, value and extent of agricultural holdings in

---

68 William Wilde died on 9 Apr. 1876. 69 Froggatt, 'Sir William Wilde and the 1851 census of Ireland', pp 306, 310, 311. 70 'Report of Council on Mr Jephson's suggestions as to the census of 1881', *Journal of the Statistical and Social Inquiry Society of Ireland,* viii

Ireland were enumerated according to poor law unions, counties and provinces. Information on the number of people residing on each holding, and the number and nature of houses was also gathered. The holdings were grouped into eleven classes according to size:

1st class	holdings not exceeding 1 acre
2nd class	holdings above 1 acre and not exceeding 5 acres
3rd class	holdings above 5 acres and not exceeding 10 acres
4th class	holdings above 10 acres and not exceeding 15 acres
5th class	holdings above 15 acres and not exceeding 20 acres
6th class	holdings above 20 acres and not exceeding 30 acres
7th class	holdings above 30 acres and not exceeding 50 acres
8th class	holdings above 50 acres and not exceeding 100 acres
9th class	holdings above 100 acres and not exceeding 200 acres
10th class	holdings above 200 acres and not exceeding 500 acres
11th class	holdings above 500 acres

The land survey was retained and published in the *General Report* of each subsequent census to 1911.

In bound form the entire 1881 census was contained in five volumes, one for each province, plus the *General Report*, though as with the previous census, individual county books were available.

THE CENSUS OF IRELAND FOR THE YEAR 1891

Two of the commissioners from 1881 served on the 1891 census, Dr Thomas W. Grimshaw, the registrar-general, and Robert E. Matheson. The newcomer was Dr T.J. Bellingham Brady. Census day was 5 April 1891. The 'Imperial' model was by now well established though small differences occurred in a few tables. One noteworthy event associated with the enumeration was an outbreak of smallpox in the north of the country. Because of the infectious nature of smallpox there was concern for those engaged in collecting census information. After consultation with the medical commissioners of the Local Government Board, the secretary of the General Post Office, the authorities at the Stationery office and the Department of Public Works, arrangements were made to set up a disinfecting apparatus in the census office. In the event, the procedures adopted, if over zealous, did permit the census commissioners 'to state that these precautions proved effectual, and that no case of infectious disease occurred amongst our staff during the progress of the work'.[71]

(1881), p. 158.   **71** *Census of Ireland, 1891*, part ii, *General Report*, HC 1892 [C. 6780], xc, p. 2.

4 Thomas Wrigley Grimshaw, registrar-general, 1879–1900

THE CENSUS OF IRELAND FOR THE YEAR 1901

By 1901 Thomas Grimshaw had died and Robert Matheson was promoted to registrar-general. Matheson had started in the office of the registrar of marriages as a clerk in 1863, interrupted this employment to gain a law degree and was called to the Irish bar in 1875. He returned to the civil service two years later as secretary to the Registrar-General's Office, rose in the ranks and finally was appointed as registrar-general in 1900. No other registrar-general had started as a clerk and ended his career as the most senior official. Dr Bellingham Brady served for a second time. A new commissioner was Robert Brew who had acted as superintendent of accounts for the 1891 census.[72] Census day was 31 March 1901.

72 Brew was also responsible in both 1881 and 1891 for the preparation of housing statistics, and was compiler in 1891 of a census of the Irish townlands.

While the presentation of the 1901 census was unchanged, a great deal of work was necessary to arrange the statistics according to the new territorial units of county electoral divisions, county districts and district electoral divisions, formed by the Local Government (Ireland) Act, 1898. The ancient units of the barony and parish ceased to be used as key territorial networks, though poor law unions and electoral divisions survived, the latter renamed district electoral divisions (DEDs). Townlands too survived though they had to be regrouped to conform to poor law union boundaries and their subdivisions of dispensary districts and district electoral divisions. Consequently a new topographical index had to be prepared before the enumeration could begin.

THE CENSUS OF IRELAND FOR THE YEAR 1911

The 1911 census was the last to count the population of the entire island of Ireland. A fresh team was in charge. The three commissioners were the registrar-general, Sir William J. Thompson, a doctor by profession, the assistant registrar-general, Daniel S. Doyle, a lawyer, and Edward O'Farrell. The 2 April 1911 was census day. The 1901 census plan was used with slight modification. A major addition to the 1911 was the inclusion of three new questions. These asked about the 'duration of marriage', the 'number of children born to the existing marriage', and the 'number of children living'. Interest in the birth rate was prompted by declining rates in France, England and Scotland, whereas in Ireland there was a 'slightly upward tendency' during the previous twenty years.[73]

CONCLUSION

The first Irish census of 1813–5 was a miserable failure. The 1821 and 1831, by contrast, were successes, although they had their flaws. Thanks to the work of Larcom and Wilde, the 1841 census was a triumph. Even greater heights were scaled with the mammoth census of 1851. By now the Irish work was in the mainstream of European census-taking, and Irish commissioners were influenced by the discussions at International Statistical Congresses held at periodic intervals from 1853. The collection, organization and presentation of social surveys were high on their agendas for debate. In 1887, at the International Statistical Congress in Vienna, Thomas Grimshaw described the Irish census as 'one of the most detailed and minute in the world and therefore affords specimens of methods of working which are applicable in almost any country'.[74]

73 William J. Thompson, 'The development of the Irish Census', *Journal of the Statistical and Social Inquiry Society of Ireland*, xii (1911), p. 483.   74 Thomas Wrigley Grimshaw, *On the methods of drawing up census returns* (Vienna, 1887), p. 1.

The legacy of a census is the enumerators' returns and published reports. Most of the nineteenth-century enumerators' books for Ireland no longer exist,[75] and so our inheritance is the published reports. The subsequent chapters are designed to aid researchers through these works. The maze of administrative units used in successive censuses is explained in the next chapter, followed by a close scrutiny of a select number of themes. The final chapter reviews the work of a number of historians who have written about various aspects of the censuses. It also points to several studies based on census material as examples of what can be done.

75 See Chapter 4 for details on the surviving enumerators' returns.

CHAPTER 2

A place in time: territorial units in the censuses of Ireland

Census data are presented in a variety of territorial units. Deciding on which units would be used for assembling the information was a key stage in the design and organization of every census. The starting point in 1821 was a list containing all the sub-divisions of the country used for the collection of local taxes. The largest units were the four provinces – Leinster, Munster, Ulster and Connaught. These provinces were divided into 32 counties, 12 in Leinster, 6 in Munster, 9 in Ulster and 5 in Connaught. Within the counties were baronies, the number varying from census to census (see Appendix I). Parishes were smaller than baronies, while the smallest unit of all was the townland.

Other territorial networks were also used. Poor law unions and their sub-units, electoral divisions, appeared in 1851 for the first time and remained in use until 1911. By 1871 registration counties, superintendent registrars' districts, and registrars' districts were in place. These formed the territorial units for administering the civil registration of births, deaths and marriages. Dispensary districts constituted another spatial system, and were employed for the first time in the 1871 census. Finally, the Local Government Act of Ireland (1898) inaugurated another new territorial network that was used for the first time in the 1901 census. The new administrative units were county electoral divisions, county districts (urban and rural), and the smallest units called district electoral divisions (DED).

From time to time other administrative units such as parliamentary boroughs, ecclesiastical dioceses and petty session districts were employed. Parliamentary boroughs were areas that returned members of parliament; petty session districts were used for administrating local justice; and ecclesiastical dioceses marked the territorial jurisdiction of bishops. There were two sets of diocesan units, one for the Church of Ireland and another for the Roman Catholic Church. Parliamentary boroughs appeared from 1841, petty sessions were introduced in 1871 and diocesan units were used from 1861 to display data on religious profession.[1] A few territorial units have not been referred to, because they appeared infrequently or were of lesser significance. Finally, data on many themes were arranged according to civic and rural districts within a county.

---

[1] From 1881 separate tables for the two sets of diocesan units – Established church and Roman Catholic – were recorded with retrospective data for 1861 and 1871.

Some statistics on themes, such as population, were published at several territorial levels; others only appeared at one spatial unit. Furthermore there were variations over time. For example, population statistics were recorded at county level in every census from 1821 to 1911, at barony and parish levels from 1821 to 1891, at townland level from 1841 to 1911, and at poor law union level from 1851 to 1911. Occupational statistics appeared at the levels of county, large cities and towns in every census from 1821 to 1911. Occupational data were also broken down to poor law union level and principal towns in 1871, 1881 and 1891, but these units were replaced by county districts and towns of 1,500 inhabitants or more in the 1901 and 1911 censuses. An understanding of the relationship of territorial units to one another is essential when using the censuses, and so a short résumé of the more important of these will be explained. For details of spatial levels at which data for various themes appear in all the censuses see the *Census Survey*.

TOWNLANDS

The townland was the smallest territorial unit. The total number of townlands was estimated by Larcom at 66,700 in 1841.[2] Over time, however, the number fluctuated. Townlands varied greatly in size from just over an acre to more than 7,000 acres, the average size being about 330 acres. Originally units of land-holding in Gaelic Ireland, they constituted approximately a thirtieth part of a barony.[3] There were other ancient divisions with various names such as quarters, half-quarters, ballyboes, gneeves, and tates. The Ordnance Survey applied the term 'townland' to all of them, hence the great variety in their size. While many townland names have Gaelic origins, some are of Norse, Norman or English derivation.

Townlands were used as administrative land units from the seventeenth century.[4] They appeared for the first time in the 1841 census, and population, housing, area, and valuation data continued to be arranged by townlands until 1911.[5] Townlands formed the building blocks of several large territorial networks – parishes, poor law unions, and following the reorganization of local government in 1898, district electoral divisions. New networks and reorganization necessitated boundary changes from time to time, though the censuses contain copious notes for reference.

2 Thomas A. Larcom, 'On territorial divisions of Ireland', in *Correspondence relating to the measures adopted for the relief of the distress in Ireland*, Board of Works Series, H.C. 1847 [764], l, p. 1.   3 Ibid.

PARISHES

Parishes were ecclesiastical divisions dating from the twelfth century, though from the sixteenth century Roman Catholic and Church of Ireland parish boundaries did not correspond. The Church of Ireland adopted the medieval pattern while the Catholic Church produced its own network. Civil parishes were based on those of the Established Church,[6] although their boundaries did not in all cases correspond. From 1841 'the civil parishes as laid down on the Ordnance maps [were] adopted in the census publications'.[7] In size, parishes ranged from under two to over 200,000 statute acres and contained anything from five to thirty townlands. In Ireland there were over 2,400 parishes,[8] their boundaries sometimes crossing barony and county limits. The census enumerators used the civil parishes for the collection of data from 1821 to 1911. Following the Local Government (Ireland) Act the importance of parishes diminished. They were retained, however, 'for purposes of reference in the Townland Census'.[9]

BARONIES

Baronies were ancient sub-division of counties, their boundaries being fixed by the Act 6 Geo. IV. c. 99. Over time many were split into smaller units and a few were amalgamated. In 1821 there were 296 baronies in Ireland. But during the nineteenth century some townlands and parishes were detached from one barony and allocated to an adjoining one so that by 1851 the number had increased to 323, and by 1881 the total was 327. The census commissioners employed barony units for organizing the census data from 1821 to 1891. Between 1821 and 1861 the barony was used as the main sub-unit of the county; however, the censuses of 1871, 1881 and 1891 enumerated fewer subjects at barony level, and by 1901 baronies ceased to be used as a territorial unit for administrative and fiscal purposes. They were not, however, abandoned entirely. In both the 1901 and 1911 censuses, they appeared within the population table for poor law unions/district electoral divisions, though broken up within the new territorial structure. The reorganization of boundaries would make reconstruction difficult for comparative purposes with earlier censuses. (See Appendix I.)

4 Peter Collins, *Pathways to Ulster's past: sources and resources for local studies* (Belfast, 1998), p. 2.   **5** For the 1901 and 1911 censuses 'it became necessary ... to arrange the townlands in each administrative county, according to the Poor Law Unions, Dispensary or Registration Districts and District Electoral Divisions' and not as formerly. See *Census of Ireland 1901*, part ii, *General Report*, H.C. 1902 [Cd. 1190], cxxix, p. 9.   **6** S.J. Connolly, (ed.), *The Oxford companion, to Irish history* (Oxford, 1998), pp 426–7.   **7** *Census of Ireland, 1881*, part ii, *General Report*, H.C. 1882 [C. 3365], lxxvi, p. 3.   **8** This figure fluctuated from approximately 2,450 in 1851 to 2,426 in 1871 to 2,428 in 1911.   **9** *Census of Ireland, 1901*, part ii, *General Report*, p. 9. For detailed exposition on Irish parishes see

COUNTIES

The county was the most important administrative unit in the country. Counties were used in all censuses from 1813 to 1911. The dividing of the country into counties, the shiring of Ireland, was commenced in the late twelfth century by the Anglo-Normans. Dublin county was the first to be created, the earliest references to its existence being in the 1190s, followed at intervals during the thirteenth and early fourteenth centuries by Meath, Louth, Kildare, and Waterford, Galway, Limerick, Tipperary, Carlow, Cork and Kerry. A vast expanse of land, however, still remained unshired, and continued to be so until the sixteenth century, when a new initiative advanced the process further. This phase was completed by the creation of County Wicklow in 1606. The full complement of counties was and still is thirty-two. (See Appendix II.)

Counties were well established for administrative purposes when the first census officials were planning their task. Consequently they were appropriate units for the organization of the population statistics. However, modifications were made. The cities of Dublin, Cork, Kilkenny, Limerick, Waterford and the towns of Carrickfergus, Drogheda and Galway, were separated from their counties, and enumerated individually. The result was that in all there were 40 units, 32 counties (without the above named cities) and 8 urban centres. Over time towns such as Belfast and Londonderry[10] expanded to justify separate enumeration, while others, such as Galway and Carrickfergus, contracted and for the purpose of census-taking were subsumed into the appropriate county. In a few cases (for example, Belfast and Drogheda) the urban areas span more than one county. Other changes also occurred. For instance, so great was the expansion of Dublin city that in 1861 the suburbs were enumerated separately, forming three elements – county, city and suburbs of Dublin.[11] In the censuses of 1851 and 1861 County Cork was divided into East and West Ridings, and County Tipperary was split into North and South Ridings.

A further complication occurred in 1864. Registration counties were created, and in name and number they were the same as the counties *proper*, but in size and boundaries they differed. For this reason one cannot compare vital statistics at county level produced by the registrar-general during the period 1864–85 with the county data in the censuses of 1871 and 1881.

Finally, the network created by the Local Government (Ireland) Act, 1898, necessitated some minor alterations to county boundaries. For example, where towns had spanned two counties the boundary was redrawn to place the town

Census of Ireland for the year 1861, part iv, *Report and tables relating to religious professions, education, and occupations of the people*, part iv, vol. i, H.C. 1863 [3204–III], lix and *Census of Ireland for the year 1861*, part ii, vol. i, *Report and tables on ages and education*, H.C. 1863 [3204–1], lvi.   **10** Belfast appeared as a separate unit from 1841, Londonderry (for occupations) from 1901.   **11** This arrangement of the Dublin statistics was for 1861 only.

in the county where the population was greatest. Thus, some county data pre-1901 and post-1901 are not strictly comparable. Vaughan and Fitzpatrick have concluded, however, that since 'many of the changes were trifling [they] may be ignored for most purposes'.[12]

PROVINCES

The largest territorial units in Ireland were the provinces – Leinster, Munster, Ulster and Connaught (Connacht).[13] These had their origins in the ancient lordships. The county network fits neatly into the provincial units as no county crosses provincial boundaries. The current pattern was established in the sixteenth century, when a number of modifications took place. Counties Longford and Louth were transferred from Ulster to Leinster, Clare was transferred back and forward between Connaught and Munster, ending up in the latter, and Cavan was assigned to Ulster from Connaught. The final pattern is shown in Appendix I.

POOR LAW UNIONS

Poor law unions were established in 1838 to administer the newly-established Irish Poor Law. The union scheme was created because the existing structure of parishes and baronies was deemed unsuitable in size for the provision of poor relief. Originally there were 130 poor law unions to which was added the union of Dingle in 1848, but the stress on the system created by the Great Famine prompted the appointment of a Boundary Commission in the same year. This was composed of three commissioners, Thomas Larcom, Captain Broughton of the Engineer Regiment and a poor-law inspector, Mr Charles S. Crawford. Their remit was to examine what alterations were necessary to the boundaries of existing unions and advise on how many new unions would be required 'in order to meet the wants of the country'.[14] Originally 50 new unions were recommended, but after considerable debate, a further 32 unions were added by 1850 bringing a total to 163.[15] (See Appendix III.) During the last quarter of the nineteenth century a few unions were merged so that by 1911 there were 158 in all.

The census authorities used poor law unions for the first time in 1851 in two ways. Sometimes the data were published for the poor law union as a whole. But because many poor law unions straddled one or more county boundaries, the data were often presented for that part of the union that lay within a specific

---

12 Vaughan & Fitzpatrick (eds), *Irish historical statistics: population 1821–1971*, p. xx.   13 In the censuses 1813 to 1911 Connacht is always spelt Connaught.   14 Cited in G. Nicholls, *A history of the Irish poor law* (London, 1856; repr. New York, 1967), p. 361.
15 Nicholls, *A history of the Irish poor law*, p. 384.

county. Therefore to reconstruct values for the entire union one has to gather the data for the county or counties in which the rest of the union is located. Appendices IV–V contain a guide to the counties in which poor law unions are located. In 1871, 1881 and 1891 censuses more data were presented according to poor law unions than formerly as baronies became less important as administrative units.

ELECTORAL DIVISIONS

Electoral divisions were sub-divisions of poor law unions formed by grouping adjacent townlands. Initially there were 2,049 electoral divisions, with an average population of about 4,000 in each. Following the deliberations of the Boundary Commission they too were increased by 1850 so that 355 electoral divisions were divided to create a total of 3,404 electoral divisions. Further subdivision occurred to make a network of 3,439 electoral divisions in 1851. The number rose again in 1881 to 3,446.

DISPENSARY DISTRICTS

Dispensary districts were created early in the nineteenth century and later re-organized for implementing the Medical Charities (Ireland) Act, 1851,[16] which provided the poor with free medical care through a network of dispensary districts. These districts were formed by grouping together a number of electoral divisions within a poor law union. Originally 719 dispensary districts were created, though they too fluctuated in number over time. Dispensary districts were used for the presentation of population and housing statistics in the censuses of 1871 through to 1891, though by 1871 dispensary districts and registrars' districts were coterminous.

SUPERINTENDENT REGISTRARS' DISTRICTS AND REGISTRARS' DISTRICTS

These districts were created for the registration of births, marriages and deaths under the provisions set out for civil registration in 1864.[17] Superintendent registrars' districts were coterminous with poor law unions, and the registrars' districts were identical with dispensary districts. These new units appeared for the first time in the census of 1871 when there were 163 superintendent

16 Medical Charities Act, 14 & 15 Victoria, c. 68.   17 26th Victoria, c. 11.

registrars' districts and 789 registrars' districts. By 1891 the number of superintendent registrars' districts had fallen to 160, while registrars' districts had
increased to 799.[18] Despite further reorganization of spatial units following the
Local Government (Ireland) Act of 1898, the superintendent registrars' districts/
poor law unions and registrars' districts were maintained for the 1901 and 1911
censuses.

LOCAL GOVERNMENT ACT (IRELAND) 1898:
TERRITORIAL UNITS

The 1901 census introduced a new network of spatial units. Three years earlier
legislation had been passed to reform the workings of local government. Part of
the reform was the creation of fresh territorial divisions.[19] There were two
parallel sets of units, each with two layers. One set was known as county
electoral divisions, the other was called county districts. Both were sub-divided
into district electoral divisions (DEDs). As their names imply they were sub-units
of the county and did not cross county boundaries.

COUNTY ELECTORAL DIVISIONS

County electoral divisions were created for the purpose of electing members to
the county councils, the successor of grand juries. Each county had approximately twenty electoral divisions, and within each county the divisions contained
roughly the same size of population. Where possible there was 'proper repre-
sentation of both urban and rural populations' in each division.[20] In 1901 there
were 686 county electoral divisions. Leinster had 241, Munster, 159, Ulster, 183
and Connaught 103. In 1911 they numbered 685. (See Appendix VI.)

COUNTY DISTRICTS

County districts were composed of rural and urban districts. In 1901 there were
83 urban county districts and 212 rural county districts. Slight modifications
occurred by the time the 1911 census was taken, as shown in Appendix VII; in
the census county districts replaced baronies and were used for presenting several
sets of data.

---

18 Registrars' districts were increased to 799 by 1881 census.   **19** 61 & 62 Victoria, c. 37,
Local Government (Ireland) Act, 1898.   **20** *Twenty-seventh annual report under Local
Government Board (Ireland), Act 35 & 36 Victoria, chap. 69*, H.C. 1899 [C. 9480], xxxix, p. 6.

DISTRICT ELECTORAL DIVISIONS

District electoral divisions were sub-divisions of county electoral divisions and county districts. They were new in name only, being essentially the electoral divisions of the poor law system. To ensure that units that formerly had crossed county boundaries no longer did so, some re-drawing of boundaries had to be done. The result was the formation of 3,751 DEDs in 1901, though that number had contracted to 3,673 by 1911.

In summary, the census authorities used four sets of territorial networks between 1821 and 1911. One was based on baronies, parishes and townlands, a second set on poor law unions, electoral divisions and dispensary districts, a third on registration counties, superintendent registrars' districts and registrars' districts, and finally a set that used county electoral divisions, county districts and district electoral divisions. Some units nested like sets of Russian dolls. Baronies fitted into counties, counties into provinces.[21] Other territorial units crossed boundaries. The network of poor law unions, for instance, crossed county boundaries, sometimes straddling one or more. Many boundaries were not constant over time, as evidenced by the copious notes in the censuses identifying these alterations. Diagram 2:1 presents the main territorial units as a chart to aid in understanding these various networks.

Periodically a gazetteer was published to aid users in locating the thousands of townlands, parishes and district electoral divisions, and hundreds of baronies, poor law unions, dispensary districts and county electoral divisions, and to guide researcher through the myriad of boundary changes. The first was published in 1861 and was entitled the *General alphabetical index to the townlands and towns, parishes and baronies of Ireland*. Compiled from the territorial units enumerated in the census publications of 1851 and the Ordnance Survey maps, the volume was prepared in three sections. The first and largest section was an alphabetical index of the townlands and towns in Ireland. Each was referenced to the county, parish, barony and poor law union in which it was located. A sheet reference number was given to the location of the place on the Ordnance Survey map, and finally a volume and page reference to the statistics for that townland or town in the census. A sample section from one of its pages will give an indication of its value, shown below.

---

21 In a few baronies a small tongue of land extended into the adjoining county. See maps in Ruth Dudley Edwards, *An atlas of Irish history* (London, 1973), pp 16–19.

No. of sheet of the Ordnance Survey maps	Townlands and Towns	Acres in Statute Acres	County	Barony	Parish	Poor Law Union in 1857	Townland Census of 1851 Part I	
64	Dunmurry	460–1–7	Antrim	Upper	Drumbeg	Lisburn	III	10
16	Dunmurry	79–2–34	Cavan	Tullygarvan	Drung	Cootehill	III	89
35	Dunmurry	818–0–9	Londonderry	Loughinsholin	Ballynascreen	Magherafelt	III	239

Source: *Census of Ireland, General alphabetical index to the townlands and towns, parishes and baronies of Ireland* (Dublin, 1861: reprinted Baltimore, Maryland, 1986), p. 427. The date 1857 attached to Poor Law Unions is that given in the *Index*.

The second section contained an alphabetical list of parishes referenced by county, barony and poor law union, followed by a third section in which baronies, listed alphabetically, were referenced by county and poor law union.

A second gazetteer was prepared to update changes found in the 1871 census; this was issued in 1877, and supplements were published after the 1881 and 1891 censuses. A fresh index was required to include the new territorial units introduced in the 1901, and a supplement appeared following the completion of the 1911 census. These gazetteers are valuable tools for guiding users of the census through the myriad of territorial units, and for tracking the boundary and other changes that occurred from time to time. *Table 2:1* provides a summary of the numbers of territorial units 1841–1911 in Irish censuses.

Table 2:1. Numbers of territorial units in Irish censuses, 1841–1911

Census year	Townlands	Parishes	Baronies	Poor Law Unions	Dispensary Districts	Electoral Divisions	Registration Districts	County Electoral Divisions	DED
1841			312	130		2,049			
1851			323	163		3,439			
1861			323	163		3,439			
1871	60,915	2,426	325	163	719	3,438	789		
1881	60,644	2,426	327	163	721	3,446	799		
1891	60,576	2,428	327	160	721	3,446	799		
1901	60,462	2,428		159	747		829	686	3,751
1911	60,679	2,428		158	741		829	685	3,673

Based on statistics found in: *General Reports of the Census of Ireland 1841–1911;* Nicholls, *A history of the Irish poor law.*

Diagram 2:1. Principal administrative territorial units used in Irish censuses

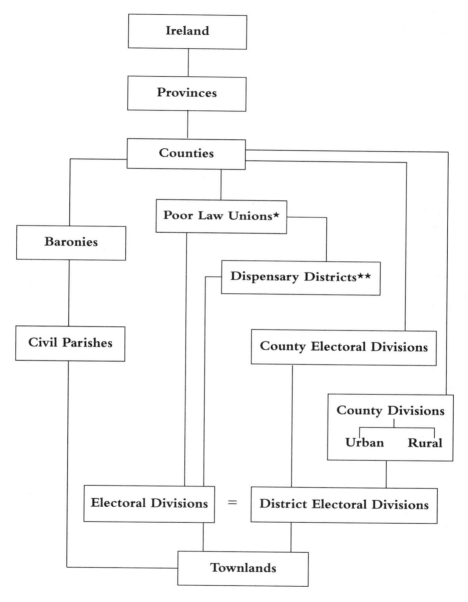

* Poor Law unions are coterminous with superintendent registrars' districts.
** Dispensary districts are coterminous with registrars' districts.

CHAPTER 3

Census themes: tinkering and tailoring

INTRODUCTION

The process of census-taking produced different types of documents. Initially there were the enumerators' hand-written records that contained the personal details of every individual living in the country on a particular date. Then followed the published report(s) in which was recorded the collated information from the enumeration ledgers into territorial units and themes. Over time census-taking expanded beyond a mere count of the people to include collecting data on many aspects of society. In Ireland the themes covered increased in every census from 1821 to 1861, the largest expansion occurring in 1851, when a wealth of subject areas were enumerated, some unique to that part of the United Kingdom. For example, only the Irish census classified the quality of housing or counted the size and value of farms and livestock, or contained a definitive work on disease as part of the census process. Consequently, the single report of early censuses expanded to eleven volumes in 1861, covering themes such as education, age, housing quality, religion, disease and deaths. Thereafter some topics were abandoned and new ones added; also a *General Report* was published for every census from 1851 to 1911.[1] From 1871 onwards the thematic volumes were discontinued with the exception of a volume of vital statistics, though even it did not survive another census. Instead there was a new format consisting of county volumes containing thematic tables.

CENSUS THEMES

This chapter focuses on the themes presented in the published census volumes. The themes can be grouped into seven categories, though not all are found in every census:

(a) People: their number, sex, age, and marital status
(b) Social groups: families and households, paupers and prisoners
(c) Education: literacy, language, and schooling

1 The tables published in the *Report of Commissioners appointed to take the census of Ireland for the year 1841* has a similar format to the *General Reports* of 1851 and 1861.

(d) Religion: denomination, literacy levels, occupations
(e) Occupations: analysed by age, and later also by literacy and religion
(f) Health: morbidity and mortality
(g) Mobility: migration and emigration

It is impossible to discuss all the census themes in this short book, but a number have been highlighted for exploration. First, we examine population, looking at the different ways these figures have been presented over the ten censuses. Secondly, we discuss the treatment of housing, not just because it was a unique feature of the Irish census but because housing quality has been used by historians as a rough indicator of poverty. Thirdly, occupations and educational attainment are also pointers to economic activity, and provide interesting insights into changes in the Irish economy over time. Finally, the presentation of data on births, marriages, disease and death will be examined.

POPULATION

The census in 1813–15 was no more than an incomplete count of 'souls'. In 1821 the population was enumerated by males and females and recorded for parishes, towns, villages, baronies and counties. Totals were summarized for the provinces and aggregated to the entire country. The same procedure was followed in 1831. In 1841 major improvements occurred. The population was recorded by gender for the smallest territorial unit, the townland, with statistics aggregated up the spatial hierarchy to provincial and national totals. A new feature was the presentation in the *General Report* of individuals grouped into households and classified into families, visitors and servants as shown in *Table 3:1*.

Table 3:1. Presentation of population statistics as printed in the
General Report of the 1841 census

PERSONS								
MALES				FEMALES				
Heads of Families and their Children	Visitors	Servants	Total number of Males	Heads of Families and their Children	Visitors	Servants	Total number of Females	Total number of Males and Females

Source: *The Report of Commissioners appointed to take the census of Ireland for the year 1841* (hereafter *Census Report*, 1841), H.C. 1856 [2134], xxxi.

There is some ambiguity about these categories. The first column seems to include parents and their children. The second category, 'Visitors', embraces other members of the household who might or might not be related. The third refers to living-in servants.

In the 1851 census, population figures were published for two spatial networks. Statistics were arranged for baronies, parishes and townlands, the figures for 1851 being printed alongside those for 1841. A second set of population statistics was produced for poor law unions and electoral divisions. The figures for 1841 were reworked into these spatial units and also printed along side the 1851 data as shown in *Table 3:2*. A similar pattern was maintained in the 1861 census, with retrospective totals for 1841 and 1851.

Table 3:2. Population statistics as printed in the 1851 census

(a) Parishes & townlands

Parishes, Townlands and Towns	Area	Population in 1841			Population in 1851		
		Males	Females	Total	Males	Females	Total

(b) Electoral divisions

Electoral Divisions	Area	Population in 1841			Population in 1851		
		Males	Females	Total	Males	Females	Total

Source: extracted from *Census of Ireland*, 1851, part i, H.C. 1852–3, vols xci and xcii.

In the 1871 census the household details contained in the 1841, 1851 and 1861 censuses were abandoned. The population categories reverted to 'persons', 'males' and 'females'. The same territorial levels as before were used though the data were presented in three new formats as shown in the following *Table 3:3*. Additional to these were the new registrars' units created for civil registration. This presentation was maintained for the 1881 and 1891 censuses.

Table 3:3. Population statistics as printed in the 1871 census

(a) Baronies

Baronies	Area in Statute Acres	Population						General Valuation of Houses and Land in 1871
		1841	1851	1861	1871			
					Persons	Males	Females	

(b) Poor law unions, registrars' districts & electoral divisions

[Poor Law] Unions or Superintendent Registrars' Districts		Area in Statute Acres	Population					
Registrars' Districts	Electoral Divisions within Registrars' Districts		Persons		Males		Females	
			1861	1871	1861	1871	1861	1871

(c) Baronies, parishes and townlands

Baronies, Parishes, Townlands and Towns	Area	Population						Valuation of Houses and Land in 1871
		1841	1851	1861	1871			
					Persons	Males	Females	

Source: extracted from *The Census of Ireland for the year 1871*, part i, H.C. 1872, vols lxvii, lxxii, lxxiv.

The 1901 population census was designed to look the same as the three previous ones, but it used new administration units. Parishes and baronies ceased to be used, and in their place came county electoral districts, county districts and district electoral divisions. Poor law unions and townlands were the survivors from former censuses. This pattern was followed in 1911.

Population statistics were also presented at other spatial levels from time to time and *Table 3:4* provides a guide.

Table 3:4. Spatial levels at which population statistics were enumerated, 1821–1911

Spatial units	1821	1831	1841	1851	1861	1871	1881	1891	1901	1911
Townlands			•	•	•	•	•	•	•	•
Parishes	•	•	•	•	•	•	•	•		
Baronies	•	•	•	•	•	•	•	•		
County/city/town	•	•	•	•	•	•	•	•	•	•
Parliamentary borough/ divisions			•	•	•	•	•	•	•	•
Petty sessions						•	•	•		
Poor law unions				•*	•	•	•	•	•	•
Electoral divisions				•*	•	•	•	•		
Registrars' districts						•	•	•	•	•
County electoral divisions									•	•
Municipal boroughs									•	•
District electoral division									•	•

* Figures for 1841 at this territorial level are available in the 1851 census.[2] See text.

HOUSING

The counting of houses commenced in 1821. The task was carried out under four headings: (i) inhabited houses; (ii) the number of families living in every house; (iii) the number of uninhabited houses; (iv) the number of houses under construction. The same method was used in 1831. It was in 1841 that a quality quotient was applied to the inhabited housing stock, a practice maintained until 1911.

The reason for measuring quality was the realization by the census commissioners of how misleading a mere housing count could be. They provided an example to justify their point. In the barony of Iveragh, County Kerry, there were 5,126 houses, 4,894 of which were inhabited, accommodating 5,129 families. After grouping the inhabited accommodating into four classes, based on quality criteria, it was found that only 2 per cent were first-class houses, 7 per cent second-class, 20 per cent third-class, leaving over 70 per cent in the

2 The 1841 population statistics at poor law and electoral division levels did not appear in the 1841 census. They were incorporated into the 1851 census for comparison.

bottom category. This information, stated the commissioners, 'would indicate …
the inhabitants of this barony are living in a very low state'.[3]

The criteria used to classify housing were the quality of building materials,
the number of rooms and the presence of windows. Thus a fourth or lowest
grade of house contained but one room and was made of mud. A third-class
house was built of mud with between two and four rooms and windows. To
achieve second-class status a house had to have from five to nine rooms with
windows, such as 'a good farm house or in towns a house in a small street'. A
first-class dwelling was determined by superiority over the preceding three
classes. The quality of housing was recorded at parish, town and barony level in
1841, 1851 and 1861 aggregated to county, provincial and national levels. From
1871 to 1911, the county was the smallest spatial level at which housing quality
was presented.

In the 1871 census, fourth-class housing was further divided into two groups
identified as A and B. Class 4A represented the one-roomed brick or stone
cabin, houses which in former censuses would have achieved third-class status;
class 4B group identified mud cabins, a type of housing that was disappearing
from the landscape. This subdivision was prompted by an appreciation of the
difference between a one-roomed mud cabin and a one-roomed stone cabin.
The accommodation and space may have been the same, but the quality and
durability of the abode were different. The censuses of 1881, 1891, 1901 and 1911
reverted to the pre-1871 classification, describing fourth-class housing as of 'mud
or other perishable material and containing one room and window'. There was
one more modification. In the county books of 1901 and 1911 second and third-
class housing were amalgamated, though in the *General Reports* county numbers
were prepared and presented as in the old formula of four grades.

Accompanying the enumeration of housing quality were statistics of the
number of families living in each class of housing. These data were presented at
parish, barony, county, city and large town levels in the 1841, 1851 and 1861
censuses and at county and city levels from 1871 to 1911. A further division into
civic and rural districts occurred for county summaries in both housing grade
and the number of families occupying the types of housing from 1841 to 1911.
In 1901 more information on housing was included. Firstly, a table was prepared
to record the number of occupiers living in less than five rooms. This
information was published for county districts and aggregated to the county
level. Secondly, data were presented of the numbers living in what were termed
'tenements of one room' at the spatial units of district electoral divisions and
county divisions. The 1911 census continued to publish these statistics.

3 *Census Report, 1841*, p. xiv.

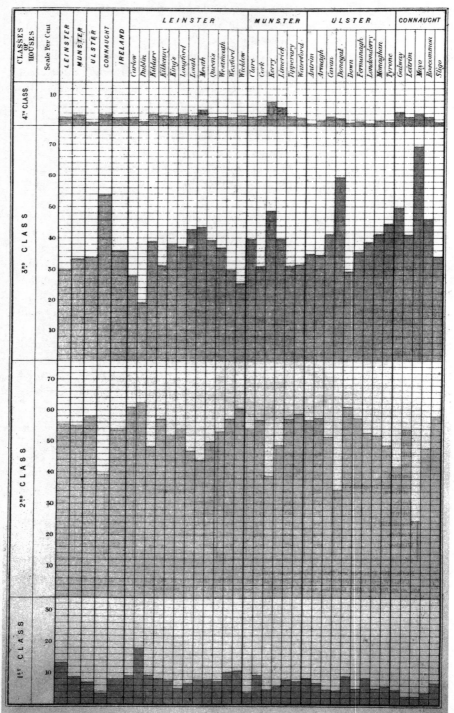

5 Diagram showing the number of houses in each class, 1891 census

OCCUPATIONS

The census is a great source of information about how people earned their living. Occupational data can be used as an indicator of social status and economic wealth. Over the decades a great deal of thought went into organising occupations into groups with 'like' characteristics or meaningful associations.

OCCUPATIONS IN 1821 CENSUS

Information on occupations was presented in 1821 as a section of a large table containing statistics of population, housing, and school attendance. The data were arranged in three broad occupational categories plus a figure for the total number occupied. What we are not told is whether these statistics included women workers. A sample from the 1821 census is shown in *Table 3:5*.

Table 3:5. Occupations of persons in the barony of Rosclogher, County Leitrim, 1821

Parishes, towns, villages, or other denominations		No. of Persons chiefly employed in Agriculture	No. of Persons chiefly employed in Trades, Manufactures or Handicrafts	No. of all other Persons occupied and not comprised in the two preceding Classes	Total number of Persons occupied
V. Rosclogher Barony					
Cloonclare (part)	Parish	955	1,057	149	2,161
Killasnet	Parish	1,791	2,087	188	4,066
Manorhamilton (part)	Village	96	238	8	342
Gortinar	Village	52	58	4	114
Rossinver	Parish	1,971	839	404	3,214
Total		4,865	4,279	753	9,897

Source: extracted from *An account of the population of Ireland in 1821*, H.C. 1824 (577), xxii, p. 345.

OCCUPATIONS IN 1831 CENSUS

In 1831 there were two occupational tables for every county. As in 1821, numbers employed in broad occupational groups were published for parishes, towns, villages and baronies, then aggregated to county level, illustrated in *Table 3:7* (see page 53).

A second table showed occupations of 'males of twenty years of age employed in retail trade or handicraft as masters or workmen'. The category should not be taken literally, for it is evident the statistics relate to men twenty years of age *and over*. Approximately 100 individual occupations were listed alphabetically, compiled for counties, cities and large towns. A sample from County Westmeath follows in *Table 3:6*.

Table 3:6. Sample of occupations from the County Westmeath table, 1831

Specification	Athlone	County of Westmeath	Specification	Athlone	County of Westmeath	Specification	Athlone	County of Westmeath
Auctioneer or Appraiser, Sheriff's Broker	–	2	Brewer	1	1	Cooper	6	185
Baker, Gingerbread, Fancy	9	65	Brogue-maker	–	9	Corn-dealer	1	24
Basket-maker	1	11	Broker	–	1	Currier	3	12
Blacksmith, Horse-shoer	10	337	Builder	–	7	Cutler	3	8
Boat-builder, shipwright	5	12	Bricklayer	2	7	Distiller	–	2
Bookbinder	–	3	Brick-maker	–	6	Dyer	2	21
Book Seller or Vendor	–	4	House painter	7	24	Earthenware, China, Pottery	2	6
Brass-worker, Tinker	5	23	Lime-burner	2	26	Fish dealer	10	14

Source: extracted from *Abstract of Answers and Returns under the Population Acts, Ireland, 1831*, H.C. 1833 (634), xxxix, p. 102.

Table 3:7. Table of occupations as presented in the 1831 census at parish and barony levels

Parish/ barony etc.	OCCUPATIONS			AGRICULTURE			Employed in manufacture or in making manufacturing machinery	Retail Trade of in Handicraft as Masters or workmen	Capitalist, bankers, professional and other educated men	Labourers employed in labour not agricultural	Other males 20 years of age (except servants)	MALE SERVANTS		Female Servants
	Families chiefly employed in agriculture	Families chiefly employed in trade, manufactures and handicrafts	All other families not comprised in the two preceding classes	Occupiers employing labourers	Occupiers not employing labourers	Labourers employed in agriculture						20 years of age	Under 20 years	

Source: *Abstract of Answers and Returns under the Population Acts, Ireland, 1831*, H.C. 1833 (634), xxxix, passim.

OCCUPATIONS IN 1841 AND 1851 CENSUSES

Again in 1841 there were two tables of occupations both published in the *General Report*. Broad occupational groups were recorded for parishes and baronies, and aggregated to county levels in both the 1841 and 1851 censuses, as shown in *Table 3:8*. The second table recorded occupations of those employed in the counties and cities, and was more ambitious than its predecessors. A basic template was prepared and occupations were grouped under nine classes as follows:

Ministering to Food
Ministering to Clothing
Ministering to Lodging, Furniture, Machinery etc.
Ministering to Health
Ministering to Charity
Ministering to Justice
Ministering to Education
Ministering to Religion
Unclassified

Approximately 400 occupations were placed into one of these classes, the number increasing in the 1851 census to around 600. These statistics were divided into four groups: (i) 'the number of males' '15 years and upwards'; (ii) 'under 15 years'; (iii) 'the number of females' '15 years and upwards'; (iv) 'under 15 years'. (See *Table 3:9*.)

Table 3:9. Sample of occupations from the County Mayo table, 1841

OCCUPATIONS	Persons 15 years old and upwards		Persons under 15 years of age	
	Males	Females	Males	Females
Ministering to Food				
Farmers	22,049	426	2	
Servants and labourers	67,133	6,215	8,941	1,777
Ploughmen	39			
Gardeners	161			
Graziers	9			
Herds	677	67	297	234

Source: *Census Report, 1841*, H.C. 1843 [504], xxiv, p. 404.

Table 3:8. Sample from the table of occupations as presented in the 1841 census for the parish, Killurin, in the barony of Shelmaliere West, County Wexford

FAMILIES							OCCUPATIONS																			
CLASSIFIED ACCORDING TO THEIR							PERSONS (fifteen years and upwards)																			
1. Pursuits as chiefly employed in:			2. Means as chiefly dependent on:				CLASSIFIED AS MINISTERING TO:														Unclassified		Total		Number not having specified occupations	
							1. Physical Wants										2. Moral Wants										
Agriculture	Manufactures, Trades, etc.	Other pursuits	Vested means, Professionals, etc.	The direction of labour	Their own manual labour	Means not specified	Food		Clothing		Lodging etc.		Health		Charity		Justice		Education		Religion		M	F	M	F	M	F
							M	F	M	F	M	F	M	F	M	F	M	F	M	F	M	F						
63	38	13	5	30	77	2	144	17	18	39	21	•	•	•	•	•	1	•	2	1	1	•	16	50	203	107	9	116

Source: extracted from *Census of Ireland for the year 1841*, H.C. 1843 [504], xxiv, pp 132–3: Same format was used in *Census of Ireland, 1851*, H.C. 1856 [2134], xxxi.

OCCUPATIONS IN 1861 CENSUS

In 1861 the presentation of occupational information changed in several ways. Firstly, the table displaying broad occupational groups, as shown in Table 3:8, retained only the 'family' section. Secondly, two occupational classification schemes were employed: that devised by the Irish commissioners and the 'English or Imperial Scheme' as it was referred to in the next census. Thirdly, tables were produced to present the occupations of the people according to their religion and age.

The application of the English classification scheme was in response to remarks made by the prince consort at the International Statistical Congress in London in 1860. The prince had commented that 'the Census of Great Britain and Ireland was not taken on precisely the same plan in essential particulars, thereby diminishing its value for general purposes'.[4] The Imperial Scheme was based on six classes, sub-divided into eighteen orders and further divided into over eighty sub-orders. These orders were:

> Professional class
> Domestic class
> Commercial class
> Agricultural class
> Industrial class
> Indefinite or Non-productive class

And the orders were:

> Persons engaged in the general or local government of the country
> Persons engaged in the defence of the country
> Persons engaged in the learned professions or engaged in literature, art and
>   science
> Persons engaged in the domestic offices or duties of wives, mothers,
>   mistresses of families, children, relatives (not otherwise returned)
> Persons engaged in entertainment and performing personal offices for man
> Persons who buy or sell, keep or lend, money, houses, or goods of various
>   kinds
> Persons engaged in the conveyance of men, animals, goods, and messages
> Persons possessing or working the land, and engaged in growing grain,
>   fruits, grasses, animals, and other products
> Persons engaged about animals
> Persons engaged in art and mechanical productions in which matters of
>   various kinds are employed in combination

4 *Census of Ireland for the year 1861*, part v, *General Report, with appendix, county tables, summary of Ireland and index to names of places*, H.C. 1863 [3204–IV], lxi, p. xxv.

Persons working and dealing in the textile fabrics and in dress
Persons working and dealing in food and drinks
Persons working and dealing in animal substances
Persons working and dealing in vegetable substances
Persons working and dealing in minerals
Labourers and others – branch of labour undefined
Persons of Rank or Property not returned under any office or occupation
Persons supported by the community and of no specified occupation

Below is a sample of a sub-order with its class and order.

CLASS	ORDER	SUB-ORDER
		In gum and resin
		In wood
Industrial class	Persons working and dealing on vegetable substances	In bark
		In cane, rush and straw
		In paper

The Irish commissioners considered it 'expedient to continue the classification of occupations … as adopted by them in 1841 and 1851'[5] and so it was maintained and enlarged as follows:

Ministering to Food
    Vegetable Food
    Animal Food
    Drinks and Condiments
    Miscellaneous Food
Ministering to Clothing
    Wool and Woollen Stuffs
    Cotton
    Flax and Linen
    Skin, Fur, and Leather
    Silk and Silken Stuff
    Straw
    Miscellaneous

Ministering to Lodging, Furniture and Machinery
    Architecture and Building
    Furniture
    Machiner

---

5 *Census of Ireland for the year 1861*, part v, *General Report*, p. xxv.

Ministering to Conveyance and Travelling
Ministering to Banking and Agency
Ministering to Literature and Education
Ministering to Religion
Ministering to Charity and Benevolence
Ministering to Health
Ministering to Justice and Government
Ministering to Amusement
Ministering to Science and Art
Unclassified

   The presentation of the detailed county occupational data was changed too. Formerly these statistics were found in the *General Report*, placed with all the other information for each particular county. In 1861 this material was still published in the *General Report* though located within the four provincial tables and national summary tables, and displayed in a different way, shown in *Table 3:10*. This table design was more efficient for presenting such voluminous material though there was a sacrifice; age bands were eliminated at this spatial level.

Table 3:10. Sample of occupations for the province of Leinster
by county in 1861

LEINSTER													
Occupation	Total (Provincial)			Carlow Co.		Dublin City		Dublin Suburbs		Dublin Co.		Kildare Co.	
	M	F	T	M	F	M	F	M	F	M	F	M	F
MINISTERING TO FOOD													
Vegetable food													
Landed Proprietors	2,221	1,081	3,302	49	28	386	198	151	134	322	211	146	39
Land Agents	207	.	207	3	.	42	.	16	.	28	.	10	.
Farmers	70,235	7,289	77,524	3,523	461	189	8	94	14	2,345	278	4,208	506
Land Surveyors	197	.	197	11	.	35	.	12	.	10	.	11	.
Green Grocers	141	456	597	.	6	95	352	7	10	20	19	4	3
Bakers	3,029	137	3,166	159	2	898	44	73	1	187	12	189	.
Victuallers	748	45	793	68	7	203	.	14	1	78	6	48	2

Source: Extracted from *Census of Ireland for the year 1861*, part v, *General Report*, H.C. 1864 [3204–IV], lxi, p. 136.

Further developments occurred in the organization of occupations by age. For presenting occupations under the English system two tables were prepared. One displayed the data in two age groups – 'under 20 years of age' and '20 years of age and upwards'. The second table grouped the information into five-year bands. Five-year bands were also used for one of the occupational summary tables under the Irish classification system.

A new feature was the analysis of occupations according to religious profession, the statistics being presented for provinces and the whole country. This was a unique feature of the United Kingdom censuses.[6] The denominations were as follows:

Established Church (Church of Ireland)
Roman Catholic
Presbyterian
Methodists
Independents
Baptists
Society of Friends
All other persuasions
Jews

OCCUPATIONS IN 1871 TO 1911 CENSUSES

In 1871 major changes again took place. As explained in Chapter one, the Irish classification was replaced in favour of the 'Imperial Scheme' and printed in the county books. Nevertheless, occupation tables, arranged according to the Irish classification of 1841, were published at county level in the *General Report* of 1871, though this was the last appearance of the Irish scheme. The basic 'Imperial' template of classes, orders and sub-orders was used from 1871 to 1911, with 'orders' expanded to twenty-four in 1881. There were four tables of Imperial classified occupations. Two were at county level, a third presented the data according to poor law unions within the county, and a fourth was for the major towns of the county. The first of these tables was a summary of the occupied population. The broad classes were presented according to four age groups: the under 20 years of age; the over 20 years old; age unspecified; and all ages for males and females. The second table was a detailed recording of all occupations, under four headings – age, religion, literacy and total, as shown in *Table 3:11*.

6 Found in the *Census of Ireland for the year 1861*, part iv, *Report and tables relating to the religious profession, education, and occupations of the people*, vol. ii, H.C. 1863 [3204–III], lxi.

Table 3:11. Table presentation of occupations in the 1901 & 1911 censuses at country level

OCCUPATIONS	Males/Females														
		AGES						RELIGIOUS PROFESSIONS					EDUCATION		
	TOTAL	Under 15 years	15 and under 20	20 under 25	25 and under 45	45 and under 65	65 and upwards	Roman Catholic	Protestant Episcopalians	Presbyterians	Methodists	All other persuasions	Read and write	Read only	Neither read nor write

In 1871 there were eleven age cohorts, reduced in later years to seven, then six, as follows:

1871	1881 and 1891	1901 and 1911
Under 10 years	Under 15 years	Under 15 years
10 years and under 15 years	15 years and under 20 years	15 years and under 20 years
15 years and under 20 years	20 years and under 25 years	20 years and under 25 years
20 years and under 25 years	25 years and under 45 years	25 years and under 45 years
25 years and under 35 years	45 years and under 65 years	45 years and under 65 years
35 years and under 45 years	65 years and upwards	65 years and upwards
45 years and under 55 years	Ages unspecified	
55 years and under 65 years		
65 years and under 75 years		
75 and upwards		
Ages Unspecified		

The number of religious denominations listed was less than in 1861 though for the 1881 census only, an additional category appeared, 'Information refused'.

In the third table, poor law union data were presented as males and females, 20 years and over, without religious affiliations or literacy levels. And the fourth table for towns differentiated males and females into 'under 20 years' and '20 years and over', also without religious affiliations or literacy levels. In the 1901 and 1911 censuses, poor law unions were replaced with county districts, otherwise the tables were similar.

Some occupations were transferred from one class to another. For example, in 1871 dealers were in the Commercial Class; ten years on they appeared in the

Industrial Class. Students in 1861 were under the 'Domestic class' (Imperial Scheme); they were transferred into the 'Professional class' in 1871, to be moved out three censuses later, in 1901, to the 'Indefinite and Non-productive class'. Between one census and the next, a number of occupations were switched from one class to another to conform to what at that time was perceived as a more appropriate category.

FEMALE OCCUPATIONS

The 1821 and 1831 censuses ignored the existence of women workers. It was 1841 before there was an acknowledgement of women in the workforce. The *Report* explained that 'having sought the occupation of every individual, we obtained that of the female',[7] and these data were presented along side those of men. No change was made for the 1851 census or 1861 census, though in the latter year over half a million 'wives' and 115,710 'widows' were added at the end of the table in a category with children, pupils, visitors and 'all others' of no stated occupation. Thus in 1841, 1851 and 1861 females who did not have a stated occupation recorded were regarded as not in employment. However, in the Imperial Scheme used in 1871 all wives, even those with stated occupations of their own, were lumped in the Domestic Class:

> Wife of Inn Keeper, Hotel Keeper, Publican, Beerseller
> Wife of Lodging House, Boarding House-Keeper
> Wife of Shopkeepers (Branch undefined)
> Wife of Farmers, Grazier
> Wife of Shoemaker
> Wife of Butcher
> Wife following other specified Occupation

The Irish administrators were not satisfied with the way the Imperial Scheme treated women's occupations. As they pointed out in their *Report,* 'nothing as it occurred to our judgement could be more erroneous in principle than such a classification.'[8] They concluded that:

> a wife of specified occupation may be a milliner or dressmaker, a draper, a governess or schoolmistress, a mill hand in a linen or cotton factory, a folder in a printing establishment, a bookbinder, or a seamstress, [and] in all these capacities ... she belongs ... to what would be called the Industrial class, while the governess and schoolmistress, or music or

---

7 *Census Report, 1841*, p. xxii.   8 *Census of Ireland for the year 1871*, part iii, *General Report*, H.C. 1876 [C. 1377], lxxxi, p. 65.

drawing mistress, would belong to the Professional class.[9] [They commented tartly] the Domestic class, however, under the [Imperial] scheme ..., abstracts, at a clean sweep, every wife of a professional or industrial calling from the class to which she is naturally referable, and transfers her to a class which represents in great part not so much a calling as a relation.[10]

The response of the Irish commissioners was to add a special section for wives at provincial and national levels, in which all those married women, returned under Class II, Order IV (Wives) in the Imperial Scheme were reallocated to the orders and sub-orders appropriate for the occupation they pursued and to which they properly belonged.[11] However, the exercise was undertaken in the pursuit of accuracy and on what was termed 'scientific grounds', rather than to assuage the sensitivities of the women concerned. In the event, the 1871 census was the only one to record the economic activity of wives based on their husband's occupation.

Another problem was the invisibility of certain working women in the census. For example, female relatives working on farms were omitted from the agriculture class whereas farmers' sons, grandsons, brothers, nephews and so on were counted. There is a vein of exploration here for those interested in the working world of women, both in identifying the lacunae in the censuses on women's occupations, and using the data available to trace the changes in occupational opportunities for women.

OCCUPATIONS OF SPECIAL GROUPS

The occupations of particular groups in society interested the census commissioners. Tucked away in *General Reports*, particularly from 1881, are occupation tables of foreigners, the blind, the deaf and dumb, lunatics and idiots, prisoners, workhouse inmates, and Dubliners, of the city, suburbs and registration districts. Earlier censuses also had occasional occupational tables focused on specified sections of the population, such as emigrants.[12]

EDUCATION AND LANGUAGE

The first census to address the subject of education was that of 1821 which recorded the numbers of male and female school pupils at parish, barony and county levels, aggregated to provincial and national figures. In 1831 the subject was omitted entirely. The 1841 census commissioners returned to the theme, paying

9 Ibid.   **10** Ibid.   **11** Ibid., part i, vol. iv, *Summary tables of Ireland,* H.C. 1874 [C1106–VII], lxxiv, pp 38–43.   **12** *Census of Ireland for the year 1851,* part vi, *General Report,* H.C. 1856 [2134], xxxi, pp xcii–c.

close attention to educational attainment. They used two methods of evaluation. One was to measure literacy levels. The second enumerated the numbers attending educational establishments. The age of five years was set as the youngest age at which a person could be capable of being literate. There were three categories presented in the census – (i) read and write, (ii) read only, and (iii) neither read nor write – and the data were broken down by males and females, forming a section of Table 1 in the *General Report*. The spatial coverage was for parishes, baronies, towns, cities and counties, and aggregated to provincial and national levels as well as parliamentary boroughs in a separate section. Literacy information was further broken down by age bands in another table (see *Table 3:12*).

Table 3:12. Table showing the number and ages of literate and illiterate males in County Carlow, 1841

DISTRICT	MALE																							
	WHO CAN READ OR WRITE								WHO CAN READ ONLY								WHO CAN NEITHER READ NOR WRITE							
	5 to 10	11 to 15	16 to 25	26 to 35	36 to 45	Above 95	Age not specified	Total	5 to 10	11 to 15	16 to 25	26 to 35	36 to 45	Above 95	Age not specified	Total	5 to 10	11 to 15	16 to 25	26 to 35	36 to 45	Above 95	Age not specified	Total
RURAL	524	1,807	3,782	2,723	1,881	29	11	13,406	1,019	1,161	1,896	1,231	792	.	.	7,024	3,880	1,296	1,512	1,302	1,039	6	.	11,038
CIVIC	154	427	894	613	478	3	1	3,160	208	137	184	130	117	.	1	907	611	164	248	193	190	.	32	1,745

Source: extracted from *Report of the Commissioners appointed to take the Census of Ireland for the year 1841* (Dublin, 1843), pp 6–7.

School attendance was recorded by gender and by age (four to above sixteen years). The spatial units were counties, provinces and the whole country. Two types of educational establishments were identified – primary and superior schools. Superior schools referred to educational establishments where a foreign language was taught, whereas in primary schools 'instruction was confined to an English education'.[13] All these data were presented in the *General Report,* too.

Further development occurred in 1851. Literacy levels were still presented in the *General Report* in the same format as 1841 but, in addition, a separate volume was prepared devoted to *Age and Education.*[14] It included numerous tables, diagrams and maps specifically on literacy. Three tables on education were presented for each county, large cities, provinces and the whole nation, broken down by age bands. *Table 3:13* (a) recorded literacy by 5 yearly age cohorts. To facilitate comparison with 1841 the 1851 data were reworked into the 1841 age cohorts and presented as a percentage, shown in *Table 3:13* (b).

Table 3:13 (a). Literacy levels of males showing numbers and ages in
County Clare, 1851

Districts and Degrees of Education		Males					
		5 and < 10 years	10 and < 15 years	15 and < 20 years	20 and < 30 years	[10 yearly cohorts] ⇨	Total males
Rural Districts	Read & Write	796	4,288	5,510	7,601	⇨	30,924
	Read Only	1,384	2,775	1,637	1,647	⇨	9,747
	Neither	10,530	9,398	6,089	6,292	⇨	46,322
Civic Districts	Read & Write	128	529	580	713	⇨	3,369
	Read Only	149	247	120	116	⇨	812
	Neither	801	707	384	422	⇨	3,327
Rural and Civic Districts	Read & Write	924	4,817	6,090	8,314	⇨	34,293
	Read Only	1,533	3,022	1,757	1,763	⇨	10,559
	Neither	11,331	10,105	6,473	6,714	⇨	49,649
Proportion per cent in each degree	Read & Write	7	27	43	49	⇨	36
	Read Only	11	17	12	11	⇨	11
	Neither	82	56	45	40	⇨	53

Source: extracted from *Census of Ireland for the year 1851,* part iv, *Report on Ages and Education,* H.C. 1855 [2053], xxix, p. 66.

13 *Census Report, 1841,* p. xxxviii.   **14** *Census of Ireland for the year 1851,* part iv, *Report on Ages and Education,* H.C. 1856 [2053], xxix.

Table 3:13 (b). Female literacy as a percentage of female population in 1841 and 1851 for County Clare using the age cohorts of the 1841 census

Degrees of Education	Age ⇨	Females						
		5 to 10	11 to 15	16 to 25	26 to 35	36 to 45	[10 yearly cohorts]⇨	Total females
Read & Write	1841	4	18	23	15	13	⇨	14
	1851	8	24	29	24	16	⇨	20
Read only	1841	10	21	19	14	12	⇨	14
	1851	12	19	16	15	12	⇨	14
Neither Read or Write	1841	86	61	58	71	75	⇨	72
	1851	80	57	55	61	72	⇨	66

Source: extracted from *Census of Ireland for the year 1851*, part iv, *Report on Ages and Education*, H.C. 1855 [2053], xxix, p. 67.

The third of these educational tables presented the number and ages of the children attending primary and superior schools on the week ending 12 April 1851. A sample in shown in *Table 3:14*.

Table 3:14. Number and age of pupils attending school during the week ending 12 April 1851 in County Clare

Class of School		Males										
		Under 4 years	4	5	6	7	8	9	10	11	[To 16 years]	Total males
Rural Districts	Primary Schools	8	55	160	345	496	606	779	1,209	795	⇨	7,612
	Superior Schools	•	•	•	•	•	•	•	•	•	⇨	•
Civic Districts	Primary Schools	2	24	41	112	119	136	106	114	83	⇨	1,257
	Superior Schools	•	7	9	5	5	5	10	15	16	⇨	176

Source: extracted from *Census of Ireland for the year 1851*, part iv, *Report on Ages and Education*, H.C. 1855 [2053], xxix, p. 66. Above tables are samples. Identical tables were prepared for males and females.

By 1861 the report on *Age and Education* stretched to two volumes. Volume I contained data on literacy at parish level, aggregated to barony, county and provincial figures for the provinces of Leinster and Munster. Volume II recorded the figures for Ulster and Connaught. This volume also included figures for literacy levels in parliamentary boroughs, civic and rural districts organized by county. A comparative table was published in volume II showing literacy levels by county for the censuses of 1841, 1851 and 1861.

The final section of the second volume on education analysed school attendance in numerous ways. As before, attendance at primary and superior schools was recorded and for this census the week selected was 13 April 1861. In addition, data were collected on the numbers of pupils attending the various kinds of educational establishments – private, national, convent and so on. The number of days in one year (from 1 April 1860 to 31 May 1861) pupils attended school or college (under 5 days, 5 days and under 20 days, up to 300 days and upwards) was also analysed and published.

The reorganization of the Irish census in 1871 established a new pattern for displaying educational data that was maintained until 1911. Separate volumes on education were abandoned, and in their place a series of tables were published in the county books. Data on attendance at education establishments and literacy levels were combined with religious profession and age. Literacy levels were also incorporated into the county occupational tables. The measuring of literacy by barony was abandoned, though parish analysis was retained until 1891, aggregated to county level. In 1901 parish data were replaced by data for county districts, district electoral divisions, parliamentary divisions, towns and county. The 1911 census followed the same pattern. To aid in the identifying the various spatial unit used see *Table 3:15*.

Table 3:15. Spatial levels at which literacy was enumerated

Year	Parishes	Baronies	Parliamentary Boroughs/ Divisions	Counties /Cities	Provinces	County Districts	DED	Ireland
1841	•	•	•	•	•			•
1851	•	•	•	•	•			•
1861	•	•	•	•	•			•
1871	•		•	•	•			•
1881	•		•	•	•			•
1891	•		•	•	•			•
1901			•	•	•	•	•	•
1911			•	•	•	•	•	•

The age bands used to present certain literacy data did not stay constant from census to census as demonstrated in *Table 3:16*.

Table 3:16. Literacy levels by age cohorts

Year												
1841	5 to 10	11 to 15	16 to 25	26 to 35	36 to 45	46 to 55	56 to 65	66 to 75	76 to 85	86 to 95		Above 95
1851*	5&<10	10&<15	15&<20	20&<30	30&<40	40&<50	50&<60	60&<70	70&<80	80&<90		90 & upwards
	5 to 10	11 to 15	16 to 25	26 to 35	36 to 45	46 to 55	56 to 65	66 to 75	76 to 85	86 to 95		Above 95
1861	<1 year	1 & <5	5 & <10	10 &<15	15 &<20	20 &<25	25 &<30	30 &<35	35 &<40	40&<45	to	100 &s upward
1871	<7 years	7& <12	12& <20	20& <40	40 & upwards							
1881	<7 years	7& <12	12& <20	20& <40	40 & upwards							
1891	<7 years	7& <9	9 & <12	12& <20	20& <40	40 & upwards						
1901	<3 years	3& <5	5& <6	6& <9	9& <11	11&<14	14&<15	15&<18	18&<21	21&<40	to	40 & upwards
1911	<3 years	3& <5	5& <6	6& <9	9& <11	11&<14	14&<15	15&<18	18&<21	21&<40	to	40 & upwards

* Two sets of age cohorts prepared for 1851. Only includes the main tables. Some smaller tables have different age bands.

Focus on the illiterate commenced in 1841, when an analytical approach to the issue appeared in the preface to the *General Report*. Interest continued with detailed analysis prepared for the education volumes of the 1851 and 1861 censuses. The changes implemented in 1871 reduced the amount of information gathered on illiteracy. Nevertheless, tables were prepared showing the number of illiterates, and what percentage these represented of the population aged five years and over. These statistics were compiled for parishes and counties aggregated up to provincial and national levels. This pattern was repeated for every census year to 1911, though in that year the ability to read and write was measured from nine years of age.

LANGUAGE

The 1851 census was the first to seek information on spoken languages. As the *General Report* explains, 'the person filling the return [was required] to add the word "*Irish*" to the name of each persons *who speaks Irish, but who cannot speak English*, and the words "*Irish and English*" to the names of those *who can speak both the Irish and English languages*'.[15] The spatial presentation was consistent from 1851 to 1891, the data being prepared at barony level and aggregated to county, provincial and national statistics (see *Table 3:17*). In the 1901 and 1911 censuses, baronies were replaced by county districts and for the 1911 census the statistics were presented down to district electoral division level.

15 Ibid., part vi, *General Report*, p. xlvi.

Table 3:17. Spatial levels at which language was enumerated

Year	Baronies	Counties /Cities	Provinces	County Districts	DED	Ireland
1851	•	•	•			•
1861	•	•	•			•
1871	•	•	•			•
1881	•	•	•			•
1891	•	•	•			•
1901		•	•	•		•
1911		•	•	•	•	•

There was greater variation in the grouping of age cohorts over time as shown in *Table 3:18.*

Table 3:18. Age cohorts used in language tables of censuses 1851–1911

1851	1861	1871–91	1901–1911 (county districts)	1911 (DED)
1 and under 10 years	Under 5 years	Under 10 years	Under 3 years	Under 3 years
10 and under 20 years	5 and under 10 years	10 and under 20 years	3 and under 10 years	3 and under 6 years
20 and under 30 years	10 and under15 years	20 and under 30 years	10 and under 18 years	6 and under 9 years
30 and under 40 years	15 and under 20 years	30 and under 40 years	18 and under 30 years	9 and under 10 years
40 and under 50 years	20 and under 25 years	40 and under 50 years	30 and under 60 years	10 and under 15 years
50 and under 60 years	25 and under 30 years	50 and under 60 years	60 and upwards	15 and under 18 years
60 and under 70 years	30 and under 35 years	60 and under 70 years		18 and under 21 years
70 and under 80 years	35 and under 40 years	70 and under 80 years		21 and under 30 years
80 and under 90 years	40 and under 45 years	80 and under 90 years		30 and under 40 years
90 and under 100 years	45 and under 50 years	90 and under 100 years		40 and under 60 years
100 years and upwards	50 and under 55 years	100 years and upwards		60 and upwards
Age not specified	55 and under 60 years	Age not specified		
	60 and under 65 years			
	65 and under 70 years			
	70 and under 75 years			
	75 and under 80 years			
	80 and under 85 years			
	85 and under 90 years			
	90 and under 95 years			
	95 and under 100 years			
	100 years and upwards			
	Age not specified			

In 1851 and 1861 the data were presented at several spatial levels as follows: baronies, cities and towns, further arranged into civic and rural districts, and aggregated to counties and provinces. From the 1871 census onwards, rural and civic district enumeration was dispensed with, though the information was still collected for baronies and aggregated to county and provincial levels, and continued to be so in 1881 and 1891. In 1901 and 1911 county districts replaced baronies and the smaller unit of the district electoral division was included in 1911. In both censuses these units were grouped into counties and provinces.

BIRTHS AND MARRIAGES

Before the civil registration of births, deaths and marriages commenced in 1864, the census was a useful source of this information. The 1841 census included annual birth statistics from 1832 to 1840[16] extracted from the household returns, 'in the hope of forming a tolerable approximation'.[17] The results are published for counties, cities and large towns, distinguishing civic from rural districts. Similar tables were not compiled for either the 1851 or 1861 census. The crisis of the Great Famine, when many families emigrated and many more were wiped out by disease and starvation, rendered any estimate of births from the 1851 census returns spurious. Since emigration was still high during the 1850s, there was no point in trying to compile births from the 1861 returns either. By 1864 compulsory registration resulted in annual publication of the number of births by the Registrar-General's Office. Henceforth only the total number of births in poor law unions (superintendent registrars' districts), and counties for the previous ten years were recorded in the censuses from 1871 to 1911.[18]

Marriage was subjected to particular scrutiny in the censuses of 1841 and 1911. In 1841 age at marriage, the number of children resulting from the marriage and whether a spouse had been married before were recorded for every year from 1830 to 1840. Seventy years later conjugal status was again put under similar intense inspection. For the *General Report* a series of tables was prepared on the duration of marriage, the number of children born alive and the number of dead children for the county boroughs of Ireland (Dublin, Belfast, Cork, Londonderry, Limerick and Waterford), for the Dublin Registration Area, for the county borough of Belfast, and for the whole country. Twelve bands for the duration of the marriage were identified:

---

16 Birth statistics appear in the *General Report*, 1841, pp 458–9 from 1832 to 1841 up to 6 June.   **17** *Census Report, 1841*, p. xl.   **18** These data were compiled from the registrar-general's statistics. In the census of 1871 recorded births spanned the seven years from 1864 (when civil registration commenced in Ireland).

< 1 year duration	10 years and under 15 years duration
1 year and under 2 years duration	15 years and under 20 years duration
2 years and under 3 years duration	20 years and under 25 years duration
3 years and under 4 years duration	25 years and under 30 years duration
4 years and under 5 years duration	30 years and under 35 years duration
5 years and under 10 years duration	All and under 35 years duration

There were seven age bands of wives and nine for husbands:

Wives

Under 20 years
20 years and under 25 years
25 years and under 30 years
30 years and under 35 years
35 years and under 40 years
40 years and under 45 years
45 years and under 50 years

Husbands

Under 20 years
20 years and under 25 years
25 years and under 30 years
30 years and under 35 years
35 years and under 40 years
40 years and under 45 years
45 years and under 50 years
50 years and under 55 years
55 years and upwards

Less detailed statistics on conjugal status were presented in every census from 1841. At county level and from 1871 also for poor law unions the numbers of unmarried, married and widowed were recorded, differentiated by rural and civic districts for the censuses of 1841 to 1861. In the censuses of 1871 to 1891 a table was included to show the ages of husbands and their wives. The age bands of conjugal tables changed over time too as shown in *Table 3:19*.

Table 3:19. Age bands of conjugal tables 1841 to 1911

1841 census	1851 census	1861 census	1871–1891 census	1901 and 1911
County	County	County	PLU & County	PLU & County
Under 17 years	Under 17 years	Under 15 years	Under 15 years	Under 15 years
17 to 25 years	17 to 24 years	15 to 19 years	15 to 19 years	15 to 19 years
26 to 35 years	25 to 34 years	20 to 24 years	20 to 24 years	20 to 24 years
36 to 45 years	35 to 44 years	25 to 29 years	25 to 29 years	25 to 34 years
46 to 55 years	45 to 54 years	30 to 34 years	30 to 34 years	35 to 44 years
Above 55 years	Above 54 years	35 to 39 years	35 to 39 years	45 to 54 years
Ages not specified	Ages not specified	40 to 44 years	40 to 44 years	55 to 64 years
		45 to 49 years	45 to 49 years	65 to 74 years
		50 to 54 years	50 to 54 years	75 to 84 years
		55 to 59 years	55 to 59 years	85 to 94 years
		60 to 64 years	60 to 64 years	95 to 99 years
		65 to 69 years	65 to 69 years	100 and upwards
		70 to 74 years	70 to 74 years	
		75 to 79 years	75 to 79 years	
		80 to 84 years	80 to 84 years	
		85 to 89 years	85 to 89 years	
		90 and upwards	90 to 94 years	
		Ages not specified	95 to 99 years	
			100 and upwards	
			Ages not specified	

DISEASE AND DEATHS

The authority behind the presentation of morbidity and mortality data for the Irish census was William Wilde. He analysed diseases for the first time in 1851 in his *Report on the status of disease.*[19] Wilde identified nine categories of infirmity. There were four classes of physical and mental handicaps – (a) deaf and dumb; (b) blind; (c) lame and decrepit; and (d) what contemporaries described as lunatic and idiotic. There were a further five categories – the sick at home, the sick in workhouses, in hospitals, in prisons, and in asylums. These sick people were defined as 'those labouring under temporary or permanent disease'. For each section of the various handicaps, numerous tables were prepared to present the data by several indices such as age, occupation and institutional establishments. The presentation of disease statistics for institutions followed a similar pattern.

19 *The Census of Ireland for the year 1851*, part iii, *Report on the status of disease*, H.C. 1854 [1765], lviii.

For statistics on the incidence of diseases, as enumerated on the night of 30 March 1851, among the sick in their own homes a series of tables was prepared and placed in an appendix. Just over 100 diseases or unhealthy conditions were listed, and the data were broken down by province and for the entire country, further analysed by civic and rural districts, and by institutions, such as the workhouses and hospitals. Major morbidity statistics were also prepared by age bands and for counties, cities, and large towns, the data being aggregated to provincial level. The pattern established in 1851 was followed in both the 1861 and 1871 censuses, though by 1861 the report and tables on disease no longer were contained in a separate book, but were bound together with mortality and entitled *Vital statistics*.[20]

From 1881 there was a reduction in the recording and presentation of morbidity data. The county books contained two tables on morbidity. One showed the numbers of blind, deaf, dumb, idiots, lunatics and sick. The other analysed statistics on the infirm according to age and sex. More detailed morbidity data were moved to the *General Reports* where ailments were marshalled into broad disease classification groups, similar but not identical to those used by the Registrar General's Office for presenting annual county mortality data.

Table 3:20. Presentation of morbidity statistics in censuses from 1881 (for census day)

Zymotic Diseases										Constitutional Diseases		Local Diseases								Developmental Diseases					
Smallpox	Measles	Scarlatina	Diphtheria	Whooping-cough	Fever	Diarrhoea Dysentery	Cholera	Rheumatism	Other Zymotic	Consumption	Others	Nervous System	Circulatory Organs	Respiratory Organs	Digestive Organs	Urinary Organs	Generative Organs	Organs of Locomotion	Integumentary System[21]	Childbirth	Debility, Old Age	Others	Injuries	Unspecified or Ill-defined

---

20 *Census of Ireland,* 1871, part ii, *Vital statistics,* H.C. 1873 [C. 876], lxxii.   **21** Integumentary and tegumentary both indicate diseases of the skin.

Turning to mortality, it was the subject of a report first in the 1841 census when information was sought on 'all deaths during the preceding decade in existing families'.[22] For the exercise Wilde devised a disease classification scheme of ten groups into which he fitted over ninety ailments and other causes of death:

(i) Epidemic, Endemic, and Contagious Diseases
(ii) Sporadic Diseases of the Nervous System
(iii) Sporadic Diseases of the Respiratory and Circulating Organs
(iv) Sporadic Diseases of the Digestive Organs
(v) Sporadic Diseases of the Urinary Organs
(vi) Sporadic Diseases [of the] Generative Organs
(vii) Sporadic Diseases [of the] Locomotive [of bones and joints] Organs
(viii) Sporadic Diseases [of the] Tegumentary [of the skin] System
(ix) Diseases of Uncertain Seat
(x) Violent or Sudden Deaths

Wilde also created a table showing the popular names for medical conditions, together with the Irish equivalents and the English translation of the Irish.[23] Thus 'scofula' becomes the 'king's evil' in English and '*easbaibh braghad*' in Irish, which translates as 'deficiency in the neck'. This table was accompanied by a detailed report providing a brief history of individual diseases in Ireland, their geographical distribution during the 1830s, and summary mortality statistics of individual diseases.

Mortality data were presented in three tables. Two enumerated the causes of deaths for the counties, cities and large towns. One of these two tables recorded mortality for each year from 1831–2 to 6 June 1841.[24] This table had three parts: (a) rural and civic districts, (b) hospital and sanitary institutions and (c) general summary. The second table recorded deaths by age and disease during the ten years ending 6 June 1841. The third was a table of deaths by year (1831–2 to 1841) and age without defining cause of disease.

Wilde's plans for the 1851 census were even more ambitious. He compiled two volumes devoted to deaths.[25] The first was primarily an historical record of famine, disease and deaths from earliest times to the Great Famine. The work was divided into eight sections. The introduction of the first section was a bibliographical essay on the sources Wilde used in the preparation of his report. Then followed a comprehensive table of 'Cosmical Phenomena, Epizootics,

22 Froggatt, 'The demographic work of Sir William Wilde', p. 213.   **23** A nosological table also appears in *The Census of Ireland for the year 1851*, part iii, *Report on the status of disease*, H.C. 1854 [1765], lviii, pp 111–3.   **24** The remainder of the mortality statistics for the year 1841 are found in the 1851 census.   **25** *The Census of Ireland for the year 1851*, part v, *Tables of deaths*, 2 vols, H.C. 1856 [2087–I], xxix & H.C. 1856 [2087–II], xxx.

viii

CENSUS OF IRELAND FOR THE YEAR 1841.

STATISTICAL

Of those fatal Diseases afforded by the CENSUS RETURNS, with their Irish Names, and those

TERMS USED IN THE ABSTRACTS.	SYNONYMES, ANALOGOUS DISEASES, POPULAR AND PROVINCIAL TERMS.
51. STONE.	Calculus ; stone in the bladder ; gravel.
52. STRICTURE.	Ischuria ; stoppage of water ; gravel.
53. EXTRAVASATION OF URINE.	Extravasation, (from either accident or disease).
54. URINARY DISEASE.	Gravel.
55. DIABETES.	Diabetes mellitus ; the wolf ?
56. DISEASE OF BLADDER.	Cystitis ; catarrhus vesicæ ; inflammation of the bladder, (acute and chronic).
57. DISEASE OF KIDNEY.	Nephritis ; morbus renum ; bloody urine ; stone in the kidney, or ureter ; chronic disease of kidney ; gravel.
58. CHILDBED.	Partus ; hysteritis ; parturition ; puerperal fever ; abortion ; flooding ; puerperal convulsions ; ruptured uterus ; labour ; lying-in ; lying-in, or childbed fever.
59. PROLAPSUS UTERI.	Falling of the womb ; disease between one and the ground ; a falling down.
60. OVARIAN DROPSY.	Hydrops ovarii ; encysted dropsy.
61. CANCER UTERI.	Cancer of the womb ; disease between one and the ground.
62. RHEUMATISM.	Rheumatismus ; arthritis ; rheumatic fever ; rheumatic pains.
63. DISEASE OF BONES AND JOINTS.	Necrosis ; caries ; ulceration of the cartilages ; white swelling ; bones coming away ; rickets.
64. HIP DISEASE.	Morbus coxæ ; morbus coxæ senilis ; psoas abscess.
65. SPINE DISEASE.	Morbus vertebræ ; psoas and lumbar abscess.
66. ULCERATION.	Phagedena ; scurvy ; ulcers ; scorbutic ; lupus ; diseases of the skin.
67. PURPURA.	Purpura hæmorrhagica ; the purples ; blue spots.
68. FISTULA.	Fistula in ano ; fistula in perineo ; a running sore.
69. ANTHRAX.	Carbuncle ; boil ; biles ; furuncle.
70. LEPRA.	Leprosy ; scaly eruptions ; elephantiasis ; tubercular disease of skin.
71. INFLAMMATION.	Phlegmon ; external inflammations ; swelling.
72. PHLEBITIS.	Inflammation of the veins ; phlegmasia dolens ; swelled leg.
73. MORTIFICATION.	Sphacelus ; gangæna senilis ; gangrene ; dry rot ; sloughing ; hospital gangrene.
74. WOUNDS.	Wounds of all descriptions, except those of the head.
75. HÆMORRHAGE.	Loss of blood ; bleeding at the nose, mouth or anus; issue of blood ; bursting of blood vessels ; all external hæmorrhages.
76. MALIGNANT FUNGUS.	Fungus hæmatodes ; melanosis ; cancer (of youth).
77. SCROFULA.	The evil ; king's evil ; the running evil ; running sores.
78. GOUT.	Podagra.
79. CANCER.	Carcinoma ; scirrhus ; cutaneous cancer ; chimney sweepers' cancer.
80. TUMOUR.	A lump, (applied to all morbid growths.)
81. ABSCESS.	Abscessus ; acute and chronic abscess ; a gathering ; a boil.
82. FRACTURE.	Fracture, of any of the locomotive organs (simple or compound).
83. DISLOCATION COMPOUND.[a]	Luxation (compound) ; out of joint.
84. DEBILITY, AND OLD AGE.	Atrophy ; wasting ; senility ; natural decay ; decay of nature ; age.
85. BURNS AND SCALDS.	Combustio ; effects of fire.
86. DROWNED.	Accidental drowning.
87. INTEMPERANCE.	Drunkenness ; intoxication ; effects of drink.
88. HOMICIDE.	Murder ; infanticide ; manslaughter ; justifiable homicide.
89. STARVATION.	Want ; destitution ; cold and exposure.
90. EXECUTED.	Hanged.
91. POISON ACCIDENTAL.	
92. SUICIDE.	Self-murder ; self-destruction.
93. ACCIDENTAL UNSPECIFIED.	
94. CAUSES NOT SPECIFIED.	Not known.

(Left margin groupings: SPORADIC DISEASES—continued. OF THE URINARY ORGANS. GENERATIVE ORGANS. TEGUMENTARY LOCOMOTIVE SYSTEM. ORGANS. DISEASES OF UNCERTAIN SEAT. VIOLENT OR SUDDEN DEATHS.)

None of the ancient Irish works attempt to enumerate the diseases of this country, to catalogue their names, or describe their symptoms or fatality.[b] The same deficiency in medical Nosology is apparent in those of more modern times ; and in no instance has any effort been

[a] Emphysema and Empyema, Extravasation of Urine, Diseases of Bladder and Kidneys, Ovarian Dropsy, Anthrax, Phlebitis, and Compound Dislocation, were returned by the hospitals and sanitary institutions only.
[b] In 1739 K'Eogh published "A short treatise of the Diagnostic and Prognostic parts of Medicine," in which he enumerates 91 diseases, one half of which, however, were either synonymes or mere symptoms ; and at first sight it would appear as if these were the diseases of Ireland, but on closer examination we may easily perceive that they had no reference to this country in particular, and are evidently compiled from some of the ancient Latin authors.

6 Report upon the table of deaths

REPORT UPON THE TABLES OF DEATHS. ix

NOSOLOGY

Synonymes, Popular and Provincial Terms, by which they are most frequently known in this Country.

IRISH NAMES.	ENGLISH TRANSLATION OF THE IRISH NAMES.	
Cloċ an leir, *Cloch an leis*; Cloċ ᵱuail, *cloch fuail.*	Stone in the bladder;—the urine stone.	51
Ꝼortaḋ ᵱuail, *Fostadh fuail.*	Detention of the urine.	52
		53
		54
Dortaḋ ᵱuail, *Dortadh fuail*; Lonnċraor, *lonnchraos* or airc, *airc.*	Immoderate spilling of the urine;—ravenous	55
Corᵹ ᵱuail, *Cosg fuail*; Cloċ na n-aᵱann, *cloch na n-arann.*	[appetite. Non-secretion of urine; stone in the kidney.	56 57
ḃar aᵹ ḃreiṫ ċlainne, *Bas ag breith chlainne*; or ḃár ᴅo n-aoiḋe anḋaċt, *bas do naoidhandachd.*	Death in child-bed.	58
Tuitim an ṁaclaiᵹ, *Tuitim an mhaclaigh.*	Falling of the womb;—falling of "the place [of the son."	59 60 61
Scoilteaċ, *Scoilteach*; Teinnear cnáṁ, *teinneas cnamh.*	A splitting or disease of the bones;—pains in [the bones.	62 63
Ꝛalar na leire, *Galar na leise.*	Disease of the hip.	64
Ꝛalar ᴅroma, *Galar droma.*	Disease of the spine.	65
Lot, *Lot*; or Cneaḋ, *cneadh.*	A sore.	66
Ꝛalar ḃreac, *Galar breac.*	The speckled disease.	67
Ꝼeaᴅan, *Feadan*; or Liniᵹán, *linighan.*	A tube or small stream;—a stagnant pool.	68
Meall, *Meall.*	A lump containing matter.	69
Luiḃre, *Luibhre.*	Leprosy.	70
		71
		72
Morᵹaḋa, *Morgadha*; or Ainᵹcear, *aingceas.*	Mortification;—excessive inflammation.	73
Lot, *Lot*; or Cneaḋ, *cneadh.*	Equally applied to fresh wounds as to sores.	74
Sileaḋ ꝼola, *Sileadh fola.*	Dropping of blood.	75
		76
Earḃaiḃ ḃraᵹaᴅ, *Easbaibh braghad*; or Ꝼiolun, *fiolun.*	Deficiency in the neck; the treacherous disease.	77
Ꝛuta, *Guta*; or Ꝛalar na n-alt, *Galar na n-alt.*	Gout.—Disease of the ankle joints.	78
Aillri, *Aillsi.*	The unconquerable disease.	79
Cnap, *Cnap.*	A lump.	80
Meall, *Meall.*	(*See No.* 69.)	81
ḃrireaḋ, *Briseadh.*	Fracture;—dislocation.	82
Cur ar ionaᴅ, *Cur as ionad.*	Dislocation.	83
Seanḋaċt, *Seandachd.*	Senility;—seniorship.	84
Dóiᵹ, *Doigh*, or Scolaḋ, *scoladh.*	Burned.	85
ḃáḋaḋ, *Badhadh.*	Drowning.	86
Meirᵹe, *Meisge.*	A mixing or confusing of the brain.	87
Dunorᵹain, *Dunorgain.*	Murder (old expression).	88
Ꝛorta, *Gorta.*	Starvation.	89
Croċaḋ, *Crochadh*; or Riaᵹaḋ, *riaghadh.*	Hanging.	90
		91
ḃar toirmearᵹaċ, *Bas toirmeasgach.*	Accidental death.	92
		93
		94

made to draw up a general Bill of Mortality for this kingdom until the present. The only conception of this kind arose with Sir William Petty, who, in 1683, published a small tract of " *Observations upon the Dublin Bills of Mortality MDCLXXXI, and the State of that City.*"ᵃ In the opening paragraph of this essay, he says, " The observations upon the London Bills of Mortality have been a new light to the world; and the like observation upon those of Dublin, may serve as snuffers to make the same candle burn clearer."

" The London observations flowed from bills regularly kept for near one hundred years; but these are squeezed out of six straggling London bills, out of fifteen Dublin bills, and from

ᵃ London:—Printed for Mark Pardoe, at the sign of the Black Raven, over against Bedford-house, in the Strand, 1683.

b

6 Report upon the table of deaths

Epiphitics, Famines and Pestilences, in Ireland'.[26] The table was in two parts (i) 'pagan or pre-Christian period' to 1844 and (ii) 'The last general potato failure and the Great Famine and Pestilence of 1845–50'. Small extracts from this tabular presentation are shown in *Table 3:21.*

Table 3:21. Samples from the table of 'Cosmical Phenomena, Epizootics, Famines, and Pestilences, in Ireland'

Date	Event and circumstance	Authority	Contemporaneous epidemics/ Coincident phenomena
1271	'A great famine occurred in Ireland, and a heavy pestilence.'	*Clyn's Annals.*	'A great famine over all England.' – Short.
1650	'This year and the following season the Plague raged violently in this kingdom.'	*Smith's Cork.*	'In 1650 a cloud of locusts "was seen to enter Russia ...".' Kirby and Spence.
1816	'Thus during two successive years, 1816 and 1817, the season of harvest was too cold and moist to bring the fruits of the earth to maturity. The sufferings of the poor at this period did not depend on the diminution of vegetable food only.' 'Hence dampness of clothes and of dwelling, and imperfectly cooked food, rendered the people more susceptible of the influence of disease.'	*Barker & Cheyne's Report.*	'In November a great frost in England, the thermometer 11° below zero, at York. Riots in England, in consequence of the distress. The harvest of the whole kingdom deficient by one-third ...'.
1847	Fever of a most malignant character, appeared at Armagh during January. 'Dysentery and diarrhoea prevailed to such an extent as to be almost universal; also some cases of measles and cynanche of various kinds; catarrh was extremely common, very severe, and often fatal. In February these diseases continued, and, in addition, anascarca or general dropsy was very common in all ages and sexes, apparently arising, in many cases from bad or insufficient diet.'	*Dublin Medical Press.*	'1847. Fever was introduced into South Wales by the Irish. "On landing they advanced in groups to the Relieving Officer of the Newport Union to get tickets for a night's lodging in the refuge; from this unventilated retreat six, seven or ten would be forwarded the following morning to the temporary fever hospital, as many more issued from the crowded lodging houses, tottering with famine fever."'

Source: Extract from *Census of Ireland for the year 1851*, part v, *Report on Tables of Deaths,* vol. 1, pp 79, 109, 117, 295.

26 The title of this table included 'Epiphitics' when listed in the Table of Contents, but that word does not appear in the title of the actual table.

The second section contained summaries of weather conditions, crop failures, abundant harvests and epidemics from early centuries to the Famine years. Sections three to six provided reports on deaths in hospitals, prisons, workhouses and on coroners' inquests. Section seven presented historical essays on the presence of numerous diseases in Ireland with statistical analyses from the 1841 census and the returns for 1851. Finally, section eight was a sanitary report on the City of Dublin.

The second volume on deaths recorded mortality in hospitals, asylums, workhouses, prisons and charitable institutions, as well as providing data on the mortality of the total population. The statistics were organized according to counties, cities and large towns. For each of these territorial units there were four tables designed. The first presented mortality data by cause of death and by locality (rural, civic, hospitals, and workhouses), year and sex. *Table 3:22* (a) shows a sample from County Carlow. The second table recorded mortality according to cause, the information being broken down into different age bands and by sex, as set out in *Table 3:22* (b). The third table analysed mortality according to the four seasons of the year as shown in *Table 3:22* (c). Finally the fourth table (not illustrated) analysed total mortality for every county, city and large town by locality (civic or rural), year, age, sex and season.

With civil registration of deaths from 1864, the need for detailed mortality statistics, as part of the census, became redundant, and so from the census of 1881 onwards they were incorporated, without stated cause, into a table displaying births and marriages in the county books, broken down to poor law union level. The statistics were actually gleaned from the returns of the registrar-general.

MAPS AND DIAGRAMS

Maps and diagrams appeared for the first time in the census of 1841, and were included in every census up to 1901. Four themes were chosen for mapping – population, fourth-class housing, illiteracy and property assessed on the value of livestock. A series of charts was prepared to show the age distribution of the living, ages at death, and age specific life expectancy. The use of maps and diagrams in the census was a topic of debate at the International Statistical Congresses during the 1850s and 1860s. Two issues were at stake: the popularizing of the science of statistics, and uniformity in the presentation of diagrams. While sceptical of the musings of these International Congresses, the Irish commissioners were in full agreement with the value of pictorial representations. As the 1841 commissioners pointed out, the mapping of fourth-class housing and illiteracy highlighted graphically a strong spatial relationship between the two variables, prompting the observation 'that bad house-accommodation and defective education seem to accompany each other.'[27]

27 *The Census of Ireland for the year 1841*, H.C. 1843 [504], xxiv, p. xxxiii.

Table 3:22 (a). A sample from County Carlow of 'Table I – Returns of Deaths, by Diseases, Sexes, Localities, and Years from 6th of June, 1841, to 30th of March, 1851.'

Disease	Localities												Total			Years (a sample of years)				
	Civic Districts			Rural Districts			Hospitals etc.			Workhouses										
	M	F	M&F	M	F	M&F	M	F	M&F	M	F	M&F	M	F	M&F	1845	1846	1847	1848	1849
Measles	12	7	19	37	29	66				3	3	6	52	39	91	7	5	20	19	11
Fever	140	124	264	687	565	1,252	464	533	997	3		3	1,294	1,222	2,516	121	131	378	540	509
Cholera	130	114	244	35	44	79	129	119	248				294	277	571	1	1	3	18	499

Source: *The Census of Ireland for the year 1851*, part v, Tables of Deaths, vol. ii, H.C. 1856 [2087–II], xxx, p. 182.

Table 3:22 (b). A sample from County Carlow of 'Table II – Returns of Deaths by Diseases, Sexes, and Ages from 6th of June, 1841, to 30th of March, 1851.'

Diseases	Under 12 Months		Age – years 1 and under 5								Ages – Years in Quinquennial Periods													
			1		2		3		4		5 and under 10		10 and under 15		15 and under 20		20 and under 25		25 and under 30		30 and under 35		90 years and upwards	
	M	F	M	F	M	F	M	F	M	F	M	F	M	F	M	F	M	F	M	F	M	F	M	F
Measles	7	5	8	7	5	9	8	7	5	6	14	3	4	3	1	1		1						
Fever	25	31	24	25	22	22	16	22	20	21	90	93	72	76	76	101	111	67	68	56	69	57	212	288
Cholera	5	8	5	8	4	10	2	10	9	12	30	29	23	11	10	3	16	16	25	25	26	22	38	35

Source: *The Census of Ireland for the year 1851*, part v, Tables of Deaths, vol. ii, H.C. 1856 [2087–II], xxx, p. 184.

Table 3:22 (c) i A sample from County Carlow of 'Table III – Returns of Deaths, by Diseases and Seasons, in Localities from 6th of June, 1841, to 30th of March, 1851.'

Diseases	Seasons and Localities															
	Spring				Summer				Autumn				Winter			
	Civic Districts	Rural Districts	Hospitals etc.	Work-houses	Civic Districts	Rural Districts	Hospitals etc.	Work-houses	Civic Districts	Rural Districts	Hospitals etc.	Work-houses	Civic Districts	Rural Districts	Hospitals etc.	Work-houses
Measles	5	19	0	2	4	27	0	0	2	6	0	3	8	14	0	1
Fever	65	355	306	2	103	384	313	0	35	199	199	0	61	314	179	1

Source: *The Census of Ireland for the year 1851*, part v, Tables of Deaths, vol. ii, H.C. 1856 [2087–II], xxx, p. 188.

Table 3:22 (c) ii A sample from County Carlow of 'Table III – Returns of Deaths, by Diseases and Seasons, in Localities from 6th of June, 1841, to 30th of March, 1851.'

Diseases	Total Seasons											
	Spring			Summer			Autumn			Winter		
	Males	Female	Males & Females	Males	Females	Male & Females	Males	Females	Males & Females	Males	Females	Males & Females
Measles	15	11	26	14	17	31	8	3	11	15	8	23
Fever	394	334	728	397	403	800	217	216	433	286	269	555

Source: *The Census of Ireland for the year 1851*, part v, Tables of Deaths, vol. ii, H.C. 1856 [2087–II], xxx, p. 188.

CONCLUSION

This survey has discussed examples of various themes investigated by the com-missioners over almost a century of census-taking before Partition. Many topics and tables have not been referred to in this review, such was the vast quantity. Yet one of the delights of the census volumes is the foraging and finding of material which can form the focus of a research agenda or provide a tool for further historical exploration.

CHAPTER 4

Foraging and finding: the census as a research tool

Irish censuses are of value to scholars in several disciplines. Economic, social, medical and local historians have been the heaviest users. All must accept and allow for shortcomings, imperfections and occasional inaccurate information. For example, as already illustrated, some territorial boundaries alter from one census to the next; data sets may be split among several counties as in the case of poor law union statistics; and there are a number of incorrect aggregate figures. Nevertheless, as Thomas E. Jordan has pointed out, 'there is no substantial alternative to census data if consideration of nineteenth-century matters in Ireland is to be approached at a level above the local and in a manner more concrete than narrative and anecdote'.[1] Here we review a select number of works, all of which have used the censuses in their explorations into the past.

Some historians have discussed the censuses themselves, while others have used the data to broaden our knowledge of Irish history. As we have already discussed, Sir Peter Froggatt examined the 1813–15 census, and analysed the reasons for the failure of this ill-fated first attempt at census-taking.[2] In considering the accuracy of three censuses, 1821, 1831 and 1841, Professor J.J. Lee challenged the assumption that the 1831 population total was an over-estimation.[3] Thomas P. Linehan, a former director of the Central Statistics Office, wrote two articles in the 1990s on the development of the censuses that pointed to evolution in the collection process and expansion in the range of topics enumerated.[4]

Other scholars have utilized the information provided by the censuses. K.H. Connell in his seminal work, *The population of Ireland, 1750–1845*[5] combined information from the 1821, 1831 and 1841 censuses with material taken from hearth-money returns (a form of property tax) to establish the rate of population growth between 1750 and 1845. Two of several possible explanations that

---

[1] Thomas E. Jordan, *Ireland's children: quality of life, stress, and child development in the Famine era* (Westport, Connecticut, 1998), p. 78.   [2] Froggatt, 'The census in Ireland of 1813–15', pp 227–35.   [3] Lee, 'On the accuracy of the pre-Famine Irish censuses', pp 37–56.
[4] Thomas P. Linehan, 'History and development of Irish population censuses', *Journal of the Statistical and Social Inquiry Society of Ireland*, xxvi, part 4 (1991–92); idem, 'The development of official Irish statistics', *Journal of the Statistical and Social Inquiry Society of Ireland*, xxvii, part 5 (1998), pp 47–9.   [5] Connell, *The population of Ireland, 1750–1845*.

Connell advanced to explain Ireland's population growth were a rise in birth rate and a decline in mortality. Here he utilized the 1841 census births and marriage data, and the mortality statistics from the 1841 and 1851 censuses, and he also consulted the 1851 volume on disease.

Almost thirty years later an American historian, Joel Mokyr, took a fresh look at Ireland's population growth in his work *Why Ireland starved: a quantitative and analytical history of the Irish economy, 1800–45*.[6] Like Connell, he relied on the censuses of 1821, 1831, 1841 and 1851. In particular he used figures of births and deaths contained in the 1841 census to calculate 'normal' birth and death rates and hence 'abnormal' or excess mortality during the Great Famine.

David Fitzpatrick, in his study on the decline of Irish agricultural labourers during the second half of the nineteenth century, utilized both the census of land holdings and occupational data.[7] The land census was fairly reliable, but the same could not be said of the occupational data. The problem for Fitzpatrick was that a labourer with an acre of potato land or less might well have described himself on the census form as a farmer or even as a land owner. This article is a good example of how skill and ingenuity applied to census data can illuminate a major social change.

Joanna Bourke, in her book, *Husbandry to housewifery: women, economic change and housework in Ireland, 1890 to 1914* also focused on occupational data from the censuses of 1841 to 1911 to examine patterns of female employment, and the different rates of change which occurred between occupational categories.[8] She identified incomplete and inaccurate data – for example, the exclusion of farmers' wives and daughters, and the ambiguity of occupational categories, such as indoor farm servants and domestic servants. Bourke also highlighted the exclusion of part-time workers, and, in the early censuses, the omission of recording a second or third occupation when people worked at more than one job. A further difficulty that she alluded to with using the census to delve into the working world of women is the non-recording of marital status in the occupational table of the census reports.[9]

Over the last century and a half, a number of occupational categories or codes have been designed by historians and sociologists for use as an organizational tool when using census occupational data. Henry Mayhew and Charles Booth were pioneers in the field; Armstrong[10] and Lee[11] followed in

6 Joel Mokyr, *Why Ireland starved: a quantitative and analytical history of the Irish economy, 1800–45* (London, 1983). 7 David Fitzpatrick, 'The disappearance of the Irish agricultural labourer, 1841–1912', *Journal of the Economic and Social History Society of Ireland*, vii (1980), pp 66–92. 8 Joanne Bourke, *Husbandry to housewifery: women, economic change and housework in Ireland, 1890 to 1914* (Oxford, 1993), pp 31–40. 9 This omission was irredeemable up to 1891, thereafter access to the enumerators' returns permitted extracting marital status. 10 W.A. Armstrong, 'The use of information about occupation' in E.A. Wrigley (ed.), *Nineteenth-century society: essays in the use of quantitative methods* (Cambridge, 1972), pp 191–310. 11 C.H. Lee, *British regional employment statistics,*

their footsteps. The main purposes of this time-consuming task of coding are two-fold. Firstly, it provides a device for placing many occupations which in the census are grouped as 'unclassified' or 'indefinite and non-productive' into an appropriate occupational group. Secondly, a coding scheme facilitates the analysis of change in occupational structure over time. Occupations recorded in the 1841 Irish census have been analysed according to the categories designed by W.A. Armstrong and published in four volumes, one for each province.[12] An aid for researchers would be the compilation of further volumes of occupations for the remaining census years up to 1911.

A fresh approach to the use of census data is to map the distribution of social variables. The visual patterns that emerge can throw new light on old ideas and established opinions. Daniel Dorling in 1995 published *A new social atlas of Britain* in which he applied computer technology to produce maps of many aspects of British society.[13] He used many sources, though it was from census statistics that he generated his population maps. With the digitization of Irish territorial boundaries gaining momentum, immense possibilities open up for local historians to expand the store of knowledge for their area by applying computer-based techniques to census material.

A number of Irish historical atlases have been published recently. *The atlas of Irish history*, edited by Seán Duffy, depicts in text and maps 'Ireland's long and multi-layered history'.[14] Several maps in this book use information from the Irish censuses. For instance, the map depicting the pre-Famine economy was created from 1841 census occupational material, and the map illustrating Irish speakers drew on information gathered by the 1851 census enumerators. Another example of using maps to add an extra dimension to interpreting a great catastrophe in Irish history is found in *Mapping the Great Irish Famine*. This book contains maps showing the distribution of population, housing, literacy, language, religion, various occupations, crops and livestock at various spatial levels. One of the more unusual sets of maps shows the distribution of disease mortality during the Famine years,[15] the data having been gleaned from the 1851 census volume on deaths.[16]

Medical historians have found the censuses a valuable tool. Froggatt concentrated on the 1841 and 1851 censuses, in particular, to scrutinize the monumental work of William Wilde.[17] Mark Finnane in his study *Insanity and the insane in post-Famine Ireland*[18] sought statistical material from the censuses, as

1841–1971 (Cambridge, 1979). **12** L.A. Clarkson, E. Margaret Crawford, M.A. Litvack, *Occupations of Ireland, 1841* (4 vols. Belfast, 1995). **13** Daniel Dorling, *A new social atlas of Britain* (Chichester, 1995). **14** Seán Duffy, *Atlas of Irish history* (Dublin, 1997), p. 7. **15** E. Margaret Crawford et al. in *Mapping the Great Irish Famine* (Dublin, 1999). **16** *Census of Ireland for the year 1851*, part v, *Tables of deaths*, vol. ii, H.C. 1856 [2087–II], xxx. **17** Froggatt, 'Sir William Wilde and the 1851 census of Ireland'; idem, 'Sir William Wilde, 1815–1876'. **18** Mark Finnane, *Insanity and the insane in pre-Famine Ireland*

did Joseph Robins for his history of the insane in Ireland entitled *Fools and mad*.[19] Robins again found the 1851 census on disease and deaths valuable when researching his book, *The miasma: epidemic and panic in nineteenth-century Ireland*.[20] James Deeny used the mortality statistics in the 1841 and 1851 censuses for his study on the history of tuberculosis in Ireland, published in *The end of an epidemic*.[21] Work on starvation diseases, fever and nutritional deficiency diseases, associated with the Great Famine drew heavily on the census of 1851.[22] Thomas E. Jordan, for his book on *Ireland's children*,[23] devised two indices for measuring the quality of children's lives in the mid-nineteenth century. These he constructed from statistics of literacy, school attendance and housing grade found in the three censuses of 1841, 1851 and 1861.

Foraging and finding is a particular delight of historical research. The accessibility of census material depends on what one is looking for and what library resources are available. Some census documents have survived better than others. Census reports and abstracts were presented to parliament, and published as parliamentary papers. Consequently these are available in all copyright libraries, certain government offices, the National Archives in Dublin, the Public Records Office of Northern Ireland in Belfast, and the National Library in Dublin. In addition the Irish University Press (IUP) reproduced a large number of parliamentary papers under selected themes, one of which is population. Four of the *Population* subject-set in the IUP series are reproductions of parts of the 1841 and 1851 Irish censuses. One of these is the *Report of Commissioners appointed to take the Census of Ireland for the year 1841*, selected because it was the last pre-Famine census, and so it was taken just before a turning point in Irish history. The other three facsimiles are the two volumes of part one (*area, population and housing*), and the third is part six (*General Report*) of the 1851 census. A few university libraries have some or all of the census volumes in paper copy, and many have acquired the microform version. At a local level accessibility is patchy. Some libraries have acquired the IUP series; others have volumes pertaining to their locality, though a number have the entire sets of census volumes from 1813–15 to 1911 on microform. Extracts from the censuses of 1813–15, 1821, 1841, 1851–1911 can be viewed at the following web site: 'www.qub.ac.uk/cdda/'; and selected datasets can be procured from the Essex Data Archive, University of Essex, Colchester, England.

(London, 1981).   **19** Joseph Robins, *Fools and mad* (Dublin, 1986).   **20** Joseph Robins, *The miasma: epidemic and panic in nineteenth-century Ireland* (Dublin, 1995).   **21** James Deeny, *The end of an epidemic* (Dublin, 1995).   **22** E. Margaret Crawford, 'Scurvy in Ireland during the Great Famine', *Journal of the Society for the Social History of Medicine*, i, no. 3 (1988), pp 281–300; idem, 'Subsistence crises and famines in Ireland: a nutritionist's view' in E. Margaret Crawford (ed.), *Famine: the Irish experience, 900–1900: subsistence crises and famines in Ireland* (Edinburgh, 1989), pp 198–219; idem, 'Typhus in Ireland' in G. Jones & E. Malcolm (eds), *Medicine, disease and the state in Ireland, 1650–1940* (Cork, 1999), pp 121–37.   **23** Jordan, *Ireland's children: quality of life*, pp 78–94.

The enumerators' books, however, were unpublished and as such are classed as manuscripts. They are part of a nation's heritage and the property of the government of the land; consequently they are subject to legislation governing public accessibility. The sensitivity of documents dictates the duration of closure to the public. Certain papers have a 30-year restricted rule, others have a 50-year bar and some are closed for 100 years. Governments vary in their accessibility laws. All the manuscript documents under discussion, except the 1911 census, are more than 100 years old, but only fragments of data from the enumerators' returns have survived for the censuses of 1821, 1831, 1841, and 1851, and there are none for 1861, 1871, 1881 and 1891. Complete enumerator records for every county in Ireland exist for the twentieth century. Accessibility, however, varies between the two jurisdictions. In Northern Ireland the enumerator returns are open for the 1901 census only, available at the Public Records Office of Northern Ireland on microfilm. In the Irish Republic, enumerators' books are open for both the 1901 and 1911 censuses at the National Archives in Dublin. Many county libraries have acquired copies of the returns relating to their county. An example of a study that utilized enumerators' returns is Kevin O'Neill's book on the parish of Killashandra in County Cavan.[24] The chance survival of the 1841 Killashandra returns allowed O'Neill to link this material with other local sources, such as parish registers, tithe applotment books and estate records. The result was an examination of the farming community in this parish, from which O'Neill then went on to speculate on demographic and economic development in County Cavan during the pre-Famine decades.

In the absence of enumerators' books, historians have looked for alternative sources from which to tease out more about Irish society. Certain sources may be of value either to complement the census or as a substitute. The *General valuation of rateable property in Ireland* is a good example of an alternative source. Richard Griffith carried out three valuation surveys for the purpose of local taxation. The first was conducted between 1830 and 1846, followed by another between 1846 and 1852.[25] Both of these were incomplete. Griffith's third and complete valuation survey of land and tenements spanned the years 1852 to 1864 and is generally known as the 'Griffith's Valuation'. In this survey is listed every householder and occupier of land in Ireland for each townland, civil parish, poor law union, barony and county in the country. Revisions to the survey were made periodically from 1864 to 1929. Rent books, tithe applotment books, registry of deeds records, and estate records are also rich with local information. Excellent guides for research into local history are *Tracing the past: sources for local studies in the Republic of Ireland* by William Nolan, *Townlands in Ulster: local history*

24 Kevin O'Neill, *Family and farm in pre-Famine Ireland: the parish of Killashandra* (Madison, 1984). A few surviving enumerators' books are in the National Archives, Dublin and PRONI. Occasionally others turn up in private sources. **25** See Raymond Crotty, *Irish agricultural production* (Cork, 1966), pp 298–9.

studies edited by W.H. Crawford and R.H. Foy, *Doing Irish local history: pursuit and practice* edited by Raymond Gillespie and Myrtle Hill, and *Pathways to Ulster's past: sources and resources for local history* by Peter Collins.

In conclusion, at a simple level we can find from the census reports the number of people in Ireland, their age, sex, marital status, means of employment, housing type, births, deaths, literacy levels and religion and more besides, at numerous spatial levels. It is only in the enumerators' books that information on a named individual can be found, and as we have seen only a limited number of these have survived. Fortunately, a paucity of enumerators' books is not matched in the census reports. Ireland has a rich source in these reports. In addition to the large quantity of statistical tables, the preambles to the *General Reports* of every census provide a wonderful insight into the creative process of census-taking in Ireland. The reports produced for 1841, 1851 and 1861 censuses were large works that not only surveyed and summarized the enumeration of the people, but also guide the user through the reasons for certain decisions and the mechanics of some statistical techniques. We also get glimpses of the debates at the International Statistical Congresses and how these deliberations influenced the work of the Irish commissioners. These men were at the forefront of this science and their ideas percolated through into the creation process of surveying Irish society. Even after 1871, when presentation schemes had to be brought into line with English procedures, the Irish census maintained several unique features. Irish commissioners such as Larcom, Wilde, and Donnelly set a high standard for their successors and left a great legacy for the historian.

Appendices

APPENDIX I. BARONIES OF IRELAND

COUNTY	BARONY	NOTES WHEN USING CENSUSES
PROVINCE OF CONNAUGHT		
GALWAY	ARAN	SPELT ARRAN 1821 & 1831
	ATHENRY	
	BALLYMOE	
	BALLYNAHINCH	
	CLARE	
	CLONMACNOWEN	SPELT CLONMACNOON 1821 & 1831
	DUNKELLIN	
	DUNMORE	
	GALWAY	FORMED BY 1841. FROM 1871 INCLUDES THE TOWN
	KILCONNELL	SPELT KILCONNEL 1821 & 1831
	KILLIAN	
	KILTARTAN	
	LEITRIM	
	LONGFORD	
	LOUGHREA	
	MOYCULLEN	
	ROSS	
	TIAQUIN	
LEITRIM	CARRIGALLEN	
	DRUMAHAIRE	
	LEITRIM	
	MOHILL	
	ROSCLOGHER	SPELT ROSSCLOGHER 1831
MAYO	BURRISHOOLE	
	CARRA	
	CLANMORRIS	
	COSTELLO	
	ERRIS	CALLED ERRIS HALF 1821 & 1831

COUNTY	BARONY	NOTES WHEN USING CENSUSES
	GALLEN	
	KILMAINE	
	MURRISK	
	TIRAWLEY	
ROSCOMMON	ATHLONE	SPLIT BY 1881 INTO NORTH & SOUTH
	ATHLONE NORTH	
	ATHLONE SOUTH	
	BALLINTOBER	SPLIT BY 1841 INTO NORTH & SOUTH
	BALLINTOBER NORTH	
	BALLINTOBER SOUTH	
	BALLYMOE	CALLED BALLYMOE HALF 1821 & 1831
	BOYLE	
	CASTLEREAGH	CREATED BY 1841
	FRENCHPARK	CREATED BY 1841
	MOYCARN	
	ROSCOMMON	
SLIGO	CARBURY	LOWER & UPPER JOINED BY 1831 SPELT CARBERY IN 1831, CARBURY THEREAFTER
	CARBERY LOWER	1821 ONLY. JOINED BY 1831
	CARBERY UPPER	1821 ONLY. JOINED BY 1831
	COOLAVIN	
	CORRAN	
	LEYNY	SPELT LENEY 1821 & 1831
	TIRERAGH	SPELT TYRERAGH 1821 & TYERAGHT IN 1831
	TIRERRILL	SPELT TIRAGHRILL 1821 & 1831
PROVINCE OF LEINSTER		
CARLOW	CARLOW	
	FORTH	
	IDRONE EAST	
	IDRONE WEST	
	RATHVILLY	
	ST MULLIN'S	SPLIT BY 1841 INTO LOWER & UPPER
	ST MULLIN'S LOWER	
	ST MULLIN'S UPPER	
DUBLIN	BALROTHERY	SPLIT BY 1841 INTO EAST & WEST
	BALROTHERY EAST	
	BALROTHERY WEST	

COUNTY	BARONY	NOTES WHEN USING CENSUSES
	CASTLEKNOCK	1861 PART IN SUBURBS OF DUBLIN
	COOLOCK	1861 PART IN SUBURBS OF DUBLIN
	DONORE	1821 & 1831 ONLY. BY 1841 MERGED TO UPPERCROSS
	DUBLIN	APPEARED IN 1841
	NETHERCROSS	
	NEWCASTLE	
	RATHDOWN	RATHDOWN HALF IN 1831
	ST SEPULCHRE	ONLY IN 1821 & 1831, MERGED TO DUBLIN CITY BY 1841. SPELT ST. SEPULCHRE'S IN 1821
	UPPERCROSS	
KILDARE	CARBURY	
	CLANE	
	CONNELL	
	IKEATHY & OUGHTERANY	
	KILCULLEN	
	KILKEA & MOONE	
	NAAS NORTH	
	NAAS SOUTH	
	NARRAGH & REBAN EAST	SPELT RHEBAN 1821 & 1831
	NARRAGH & REBAN WEST	SPELT RHEBAN 1821 & 1831
	OFFALY EAST	
	OFFALY WEST	
	SALT NORTH	
	SALT SOUTH	
KILKENNY	CALLAN	CREATED BY 1841
	CRANNAGH	SPELT CRANAGH 1821 & 1831
	FASSADININ	SPELT FASSADINING 1821 & 1831
	GALMOY	
	GOWRAN	
	IDA	
	IVERK	
	KELLS	
	KNOCKTOPHER	
	SHILLELOGHER	
KING'S COUNTY	BALLYBOY	

COUNTY	BARONY	NOTES WHEN USING CENSUSES
	BALLYBRITT	SPELT BALLYBRIT IN 1821 & 1831
	BALLYCOWAN	
	CLONLISK	
	COOLESTOWN	
	EGLISH	
	GARRYCASTLE	
	GEASHILL	
	KILCOURSEY	
	PHILIPSTOWN LOWER	
	PHILIPSTOWN UPPER	
	WARRENSTOWN	
LONGFORD	ARDAGH	
	GRANARD	
	LONGFORD	
	MOYDOW	
	RATHCLINE	
	SHRULE	CALLED ABBEYSHRULE 1821 & 1831
LOUTH	ARDEE	
	DROGHEDA	APPEARED BY 1841
	DUNDALK LOWER	
	DUNDALK UPPER	
	FERRARD	
	LOUTH	
MEATH	DEECE LOWER	
	DEECE UPPER	
	DROGHEDA	APPEARED IN 1841, CEASED TO EXIST AFTER 1861. ANNEXED TO DULEEK LOWER
	DULEEK LOWER	
	DULEEK UPPER	
	DUNBOYNE	
	FORE	DEMIFORE IN 1821 & 1831
	KELLS LOWER	
	KELLS UPPER	
	LUNE	
	MORGALLION	
	MOYFENRATH LOWER	SPELT MOYFENRAGH 1821 & 1831
	MOYFENRATH UPPER	
	NAVAN LOWER	

COUNTY	BARONY	NOTES WHEN USING CENSUSES
	NAVAN UPPER	
	RATOATH	
	SKREEN	
	SLANE LOWER	
	SLANE UPPER	
QUEEN'S COUNTY	BALLYADAMS	
	CLANDONAGH	CREATED BY 1841
	CLARMALLAGH	CREATED BY 1841
	CULLENAGH	SPELT CULLINAGH 1821 & 1831
	MARYBOROUGH EAST	
	MARYBOROUGH WEST	
	PORTNAHINCH	SPELT PORTNEHINCH 1821 & 1831
	SLIEVEMARGY	SPELT SLIEUMARGUE IN 1821, SLIEUMARGY IN 1831
	STRADBALLY	
	TINNAHINCH	SPELT TINNEHINCH IN 1821 & 1831
	UPPER OSSERY	ONLY IN 1821 & 1831
	UPPERWOODS	CREATED BY 1841
WESTMEATH	BRAWNY	
	CLONLONAN	
	CORKAREE	
	DELVIN	
	FARBILL	
	FARTULLAGH	
	FORE	DEMIFORE in 1821 & 1831
	KILKENNY WEST	
	MOYASHEL & MAGHERADERNON	
	MOYCASHEL	
	MOYGOISH	
	RATHCONRATH	
WEXFORD	BALLAGHKEEN	SPLIT BY 1871 INTO NORTH & SOUTH
	BALLAGHKEEN NORTH	
	BALLAGHKEEN SOUTH	
	BANTRY	
	BARGY	
	FORTH	
	GOREY	

COUNTY	BARONY	NOTES WHEN USING CENSUSES
	SCARAWALSH	
	SHELBURNE	
	SHELMALIERE	SPLIT BY 1841 INTO EAST & WEST
	SHELMALIERE EAST	
	SHELMALIERE WEST	
WICKLOW	ARKLOW	
	BALLINACOR	SPLIT BY 1841 INTO NORTH & SOUTH
	BALLINACOR NORTH	
	BALLINACOR SOUTH	
	NEWCASTLE	
	RATHDOWN	RATHDOWN HALF IN 1831
	SHILLELAGH	
	TALBOTSTOWN LOWER	
	TALBOTSTOWN UPPER	
PROVINCE OF MUNSTER		
CLARE	BUNRATTY	SPLIT BY 1841 INTO LOWER & UPPER
	BUNRATTY LOWER	
	BUNRATTY UPPER	
	BURREN	
	CLONDERALAW	
	CORCOMROE	
	IBRICKAN	SPELT IBRICKANE 1821 & 1831
	INCHQUIN	
	ISLANDS	
	MOYARTA	
	TULLA	SPLIT BY 1841 INTO LOWER & UPPER
	TULLA LOWER	
	TULLA UPPER	
CORK	BANTRY	IN WEST RIDING BY 1851
	BARRETTS	IN EAST RIDING BY 1851
	BARRYMORE	IN EAST RIDING BY 1851
	BEAR	IN WEST RIDING BY 1851
	CARBERY EAST (EAST DIVISION)	IN WEST RIDING BY 1851
	CARBERY EAST (WEST DIVISION)	IN WEST RIDING BY 1851
	CARBERY WEST (EAST DIVISION)	IN WEST RIDING BY 1851

COUNTY	BARONY	NOTES WHEN USING CENSUSES
	CARBERY WEST (WEST DIVISION)	IN WEST RIDING BY 1851
	CONDONS & CLANGIBBON	IN EAST RIDING BY 1851; SPELT CONDON'S & CLONGIBBON'S IN 1821
	CORK	FORMED BY 1841 OF PORTION OF CITY LYING OUTSIDE THE MUNICIPAL BOUNDARY; IN EAST RIDING BY 1851
	COURCEYS	IN WEST RIDING BY 1851; SPELT COURCEY'S IN 1821
	DUHALLOW	IN EAST RIDING BY 1851
	FERMOY	IN EAST RIDING BY 1851
	IBANE & BARRYROE	IN WEST RIDING BY 1851
	IMOKILLY	IN EAST RIDING 1851
	KERRYCURRIHY	IN EAST RIDING BY 1851
	KINALEA	IN EAST RIDING BY 1851
	KINALMEAKY	IN WEST RIDING BY 1851
	KINNATALLOON	IN EAST RIDING BY 1851
	KINSALE	IN EAST RIDING BY 1851
	MUSKERRY EAST	SPLIT BY 1851 PART IN EAST & PART IN WEST RIDING
	MUSKERRY EAST (PART IN EAST RIDING)	IN EAST RIDING BY 1851 SPANS 2 RIDINGS
	MUSKERRY EAST (PART IN WEST RIDING)	IN WEST RIDING BY 1851 SPANS 2 RIDINGS
	MUSKERRY WEST	IN WEST RIDING BY 1851
	ORRERY & KILMORE	IN EAST RIDING BY 1851
KERRY	CLANMAURICE	
	CORKAGUINY	
	DUNKERRON	SPLIT BY 1851 INTO NORTH & SOUTH
	DUNKERRON NORTH	
	DUNKERRON SOUTH	
	GLANAROUGHT	SPELT GLANEROUGH IN 1821, GLANEROUGHT IN 1831, GLENAROUGHT IN 1841
	IRAGHTICONNOR	
	IVERAGH	
	MAGUNIHY	SPELT MAGONIHY 1821 & 1831
	TRUGHANACMY	SPELT TRUGHENACKMY 1821 & 1831
LIMERICK	CLANWILLIAM	
	CONNELLO LOWER	SPELT CONELLO 1821 & 1831
	CONNELLO UPPER	

COUNTY	BARONY	NOTES WHEN USING CENSUSES
	COONAGH	
	COSHLEA	SPELT COSTLEA 1821 & 1831
	COSHMA	
	GLENQUIN	CREATED BY 1841
	KENRY	
	KILMALLOCK LIBERTIES	CREATED BY 1831
	NORTH LIBERTIES	FORMED BY 1881 CENSUS
	OWENYBEG	
	PUBBLEBRIEN	
	SHANID	CREATED BY 1841
	SMALLCOUNTY	
TIPPERARY	CLANWILLIAM	SOUTH RIDING BY 1851
	ELIOGARTY	NORTH RIDING BY 1851
	IFFA & OFFA EAST	SOUTH RIDING BY 1851
	IFFA & OFFA WEST	SOUTH RIDING BY 1851
	IKERRIN	NORTH RIDING BY 1851; SPELT IKERIN IN 1831
	KILNAMANAGH	SPLIT BY 1841 INTO LOWER & UPPER
	KILNAMANAGH LOWER	SOUTH RIDING BY 1851
	KILNAMANAGH UPPER	NORTH RIDING BY 1851
	MIDDLETHIRD	SOUTH RIDING BY 1851
	ORMOND LOWER	NORTH RIDING BY 1851
	ORMOND UPPER	NORTH RIDING BY 1851
	OWNEY & ARRA	NORTH RIDING BY 1851
	SLIEVARDAGH	SOUTH RIDING BY 1851
WATERFORD	COSHBRIDE	
	COSHMORE	
	COSHMORE & COSHBRIDE	JOINED BY 1831
	DECIES WITHIN DRUM	
	DECIES WITHOUT DRUM	
	GAULTIERE	
	GLENAHIRY	
	KILCULLIHEEN	FORMED BY 1871 FROM GAULTIERE
	MIDDLETHIRD	
	UPPERTHIRD	
PROVINCE OF ULSTER		
ANTRIM	ANTRIM LOWER	

COUNTY	BARONY	NOTES WHEN USING CENSUSES
	ANTRIM UPPER	
	BELFAST LOWER	
	BELFAST UPPER	
	CARY	
	DUNLUCE LOWER	
	DUNLUCE UPPER	
	GLENARM LOWER	
	GLENARM UPPER	
	KILCONWAY	
	MASSEREENE LOWER	
	MASSEREENE UPPER	
	TOOME LOWER	
	TOOME UPPER	
ARMAGH	ARMAGH	
	FEWS LOWER	
	FEWS UPPER	
	ONEILLAND EAST	
	ONEILLAND WEST	
	ORION LOWER	
	ORION UPPER	
	TIRANNY	SPELT TURANEY 1821 & 1831
CAVAN	CASTLERAHAN	
	CLANKEE	
	CLANMAHON	
	LOUGHTEE LOWER	
	LOUGHTEE UPPER	
	TULLYGARVEY	
	TULLYHAW	
	TULLYHUNCO	SPELT TULLAGHONOHO IN 1821 & TULLOGHONOHO IN 1831
DONEGAL	BANAGH	
	BOYLAGH	
	INISHOWEN	SPELT ENNISHOWEN 1821 & 1831. SPLIT BY 1851 INTO EAST AND WEST
	INISHOWEN EAST	
	INISHOWEN WEST	
	KILMACRENAN	
	RAPHOE	SPLIT BY 1871 INTO NORTH & SOUTH

COUNTY	BARONY	NOTES WHEN USING CENSUSES
	RAPHOE NORTH	
	RAPHOE SOUTH	
	TYRHUGH	SPELT TIRHUGH 1821 & 1831
DOWN	ARDS	SPELT ARDES 1821 & 1831. SPLIT BY 1851 INTO LOWER & UPPER
	ARDS LOWER	
	ARDS UPPER	
	CASTLEREAGH	SPLIT BY 1841 INTO LOWER & UPPER
	CASTLEREAGH LOWER	
	CASTLEREAGH UPPER	
	DUFFERIN	
	IVEAGH LOWER	SPLIT BY 1851 INTO LOWER LOWER & LOWER UPPER
	IVEAGH LOWER LOWER	
	IVEAGH LOWER UPPER	
	IVEAGH UPPER	SPLIT BY 1851 INTO UPPER LOWER & UPPER UPPER
	IVEAGH UPPER LOWER	
	IVEAGH UPPER UPPER	
	KINELARTY	
	LECALE	SPLIT BY 1851 INTO LOWER & UPPER
	LECALE LOWER	
	LECALE UPPER	
	LORDSHIP OF NEWRY	
	MOURNE	
FERMANAGH	CLANAWLEY	SPELT GLENAWLY 1821 & GLENAWLEY IN 1831
	CLANKELLY	SPELT CLONKELLY 1821 & 1831
	COOLE	
	KNOCKNINNY	
	LURG	
	MAGHERABOY	
	MAGHERASTEPHANA	
	TIRKENNEDY	
LONDONDERRY	COLERAINE	
	KEENAGHT	SPELT KENAUGHT 1821 & 1831
	LOUGHINSHOLIN	
	N.E. LIBERTIES	
	COLERAINE	

COUNTY	BARONY	NOTES WHEN USING CENSUSES
	N.W. LIBERTIES OF LONDONDERRY	
	TIRKEERAN	SPELT TYRKEERAN 1821 & 1831
MONAGHAN	CREMORNE	
	DARTREE	SPELT DARTRY 1821 & 1831
	FARNEY	
	MONAGHAN	
	TROUGH	
TYRONE	CLOGHER	
	DUNGANNON	SPLIT BY 1851 INTO LOWER, MIDDLE & UPPER
	DUNGANNON LOWER	
	DUNGANNON MIDDLE	
	DUNGANNON UPPER	
	OMAGH	SPLIT BY 1851 INTO EAST & WEST
	OMAGH EAST	
	OMAGH WEST	
	STRABANE	SPLIT BY 1851 INTO LOWER & UPPER
	STRABANE LOWER	
	STRABANE UPPER	

APPENDIX II. COUNTIES OF IRELAND: NOTES

Ireland is comprised of 32 counties – 12 in Leinster, 6 in Munster, 9 in Ulster and 5 in Connaught.

PROVINCE OF LEINSTER	PROVINCE OF MUNSTER	PROVINCE OF ULSTER	PROVINCE OF CONNAUGHT
Counties:	*Counties:*	*Counties:*	*Counties:*
Carlow	Clare	Antrim	Galway
Dublin	Cork	Armagh	Leitrim
Kildare	Kerry	Cavan	Mayo
Kilkenny	Limerick	Donegal	Roscommon
King's County	Tipperary	Down	Sligo
Longford	Waterford	Fermanagh	
Louth		Londonderry	
Meath		Monaghan	
Queen's County		Tyrone	
Westmeath			
Wexford			
Wicklow			

Cities and towns presented separately from the county data up to 1861 census

Cities:	*Cities:*		
Dublin (1821–61)*	Cork (1821–61)		
Kilkenny (1821–61)	Limerick (1821–61)		
	Waterford (1821–61)		
Town:		*Towns:*	*Town:*
Drogheda (1821–61)		Belfast (1841–61)	Galway
		Carrickfergus (1821–61)	(1821–61)

* In the 1861 census statistics were presented for the suburbs of Dublin separately from the city and county. These suburbs were: Castleknock, Coolock, Dublin, Rathdown, and Uppercross. They were formerly parts of baronies in County Dublin of the same name, which by 1861 were reduced in size as a consequence of a portion on the periphery of Dublin city being designated Dublin suburbs. By 1871 a new survey of County Dublin had taken place. The baronies area units were changed and Dublin suburbs had vanished, being subsumed in the city of Dublin.

From 1871 for selected themes cities such as Kilkenny, Limerick, and Waterford were amalgamated into the county statistics while for other expanding urban centres separate statistics were published through to the early twentieth-century censuses.

APPENDIX III. POOR LAW UNIONS OF IRELAND, 1841–51

	1841–9		Additions 1848–50
Abbeyleix	Downpatrick	Macroom	Dingle
Antrim	Drogheda	Magherafelt	Ballymahon
Ardee	Dublin, North	Mallow	Ballyvaughan
Armagh	Dublin, South	Manorhamilton	Bawnboy
Athlone	Dundalk	Middleton	Belmullet
Athy	Dunfanaghy	Milford	Borrisokane
Bailieborough	Dungannon	Mohill	Castlecomer
Ballina	Dungarvan	Monaghan	Castletown
Ballinsloe	Dunmanway	Mountmellick	Castletowndevlin
Ballinrobe	Dunshaughlin	Mullingar	Claremorris
Ballycastle	Edenderry	Naas	Clonakilty
Ballymena	Ennis	Navan	Corrofin
Ballymoney	Enniscorthy	Nenagh	Croom
Ballyshannon	Enniskillen	Newcastle	Donaghmore
Balrothery	Ennistimon	New Ross	Dromore West
Baltinglass	Fermoy	Newry	Glennamaddy
Banbridge	Galway	Newtownards	Glin
Bandon	Glenties	Newtownlimavady	Killadysert
Bantry	Gorey	Oldcastle	Killala
Belfast	Gort	Omagh	Kilmacthomas
Boyle	Gortin	Parsonstown	Millstreet
Caherciveen	Granard	Rathdown	Mitchelstown
Callen	Inishowen	Rathdrum	Mount Bellew
Carlow	Kanturk	Rathkeale	Newport
Carrickmacross	Kells	Roscommon	Oughterard
Carrick-on-Shannon	Kenmare	Roscrea	Portumna
Carrick-on-Suir	Kilkeel	Scarriff	Skull
Cashel	Kilkenny	Shillelagh	Strokestown
Castlebar	Killarney	Skibbereen	Thomastown
Castleblayney	Kilmallock	Sligo	Tobercurry
Castlederg	Kilrush	Strabane	Tulla
Castlereagh	Kinsale	Stranorlar	Urlingford
Cavan	Larne	Swineford	Youghal
Celbridge	Letterkenny	Thurles	
Clifden	Limerick	Tipperary	
Clogheen	Lisburn	Tralee	
Clogher	Lismore	Trim	
Clones	Lisnaskea	Tuam	
Clonmel	Listowel	Tullamore	
Coleraine	Londonderry	Waterford	
Cookstown	Longford	Westport	
Cootehill	Loughrea	Wexford	
Cork	Lowtherstown		
Donegal	Lurgan		

APPENDIX IV. POOR LAW UNIONS AND THEIR COUNTY
AFFILIATIONS IN 1851

POOR LAW UNION NAME	COUNTIES		
ABBEYLEIX	QUEEN'S COUNTY		
ANTRIM	ANTRIM		
ARDEE	LOUTH	MEATH	
ARMAGH	ARMAGH	TYRONE	
ATHLONE	ROSCOMMON	WESTMEATH	
ATHY	KILDARE	QUEEN'S COUNTY	
BAILIEBOROUGH	CAVAN		
BALLINA	MAYO	SLIGO	
BALLINASLOE	GALWAY	ROSCOMMON	
BALLINROBE	GALWAY	MAYO	
BALLYCASTLE	ANTRIM		
BALLYMAHON	LONGFORD	WESTMEATH	
BALLYMENA	ANTRIM		
BALLYMONEY	ANTRIM	LONDONDERRY	
BALLYSHANNON	DONEGAL	FERMANAGH	LEITRIM
BALLYVAGHAN	CLARE		
BALROTHERY	DUBLIN		
BALTINGLASS	WICKLOW	KILDARE	CARLOW
BANBRIDGE	ARMAGH	DOWN	
BANDON	CORK		
BANTRY	CORK		
BAWNBOY	CAVAN	LEITRIM	
BELFAST	ANTRIM	DOWN	
BELMULLET	MAYO		
BIRR/ PARSONSTOWN	KING'S COUNTY	TIPPERARY	
BORRISOKANE	TIPPERARY		
BOYLE	ROSCOMMON	SLIGO	
CAHERCIVEEN	KERRY		
CALLAN	KILKENNY	TIPPERARY	
CARLOW	CARLOW	KILDARE	QUEEN'S COUNTY
CARRICK-ON- SHANNON	LEITRIM	ROSCOMMON	
CARRICK-ON-SUIR	KILKENNY	TIPPERARY	WATERFORD

POOR LAW UNION NAME	COUNTIES		
CARRICKMACROSS	MONAGHAN		
CASHEL	TIPPERARY		
CASTLEBAR	MAYO		
CASTLEBLAYNEY	ARMAGH	MONAGHAN	
CASTLECOMER	KILKENNY		
CASTLEDERG	TYRONE		
CASTLEREAGH	ROSCOMMON	MAYO	
CASTLETOWN	CORK		
CASTLETOWN-DELVIN/DEVLIN	MEATH	WESTMEATH	
CAVAN	CAVAN		
CELBRIDGE	DUBLIN	KILDARE	MEATH
CLAREMORRIS	MAYO		
CLIFDEN	GALWAY	MAYO	
CLOGHEEN	TIPPERARY	WATERFORD	
CLOGHER	MONAGHAN	TYRONE	
CLONAKILTY	CORK		
CLONES	FERMANAGH	MONAGHAN	
CLONMEL	TIPPERARY	WATERFORD	
COLERAINE	ANTRIM	LONDONDERRY	
COOKSTOWN	TYRONE		
COOTEHILL	CAVAN	MONAGHAN	
CORK	CORK		
CORROFIN	CLARE		
CROOM	LIMERICK		
DINGLE	KERRY		
DONAGHMORE	QUEEN'S COUNTY		
DONEGAL	DONEGAL		
DOWNPATRICK	DOWN		
DROGHEDA	LOUTH	MEATH	
DROMORE WEST	SLIGO		
DUBLIN NORTH	DUBLIN		
DUBLIN SOUTH	DUBLIN		
DUNDALK	ARMAGH	LOUTH	MONAGHAN
DUNFANAGHY	DONEGAL		
DUNGANNON	TYRONE		
DUNGARVAN	WATERFORD		

POOR LAW UNION NAME	COUNTIES		
DUNMANWAY	CORK		
DUNSHAUGHLIN	DUBLIN	MEATH	
EDENDERRY	KILDARE	KING'S COUNTY	MEATH
ENNIS	CLARE		
ENNISCORTHY	CARLOW	WEXFORD	
ENNISKILLEN	CAVAN	FERMANAGH	TYRONE
ENNISTIMON	CLARE		
FERMOY	CORK		
GALWAY	GALWAY		
GLENNAMADDY	GALWAY	ROSCOMMON	
GLENTIES	DONEGAL		
GLIN	KERRY	LIMERICK	
GOREY	WEXFORD		
GORT	CLARE	GALWAY	
GORTIN	TYRONE		
GRANARD	CAVAN	LONGFORD	WESTMEATH
INISHOWEN	DONEGAL		
KANTURK	CORK	LIMERICK	
KELLS	CAVAN	MEATH	
KENMARE	KERRY		
KILKEEL	DOWN		
KILKENNY	KILKENNY		
KILLADYSERT	CLARE		
KILLALA	MAYO		
KILLARNEY	KERRY		
KILMACTHOMAS	WATERFORD		
KILMALLOCK	CORK	LIMERICK	
KILRUSH	CLARE		
KINSALE	CORK		
LARNE	ANTRIM		
LETTERKENNY	DONEGAL		
LIMERICK	CLARE	LIMERICK	
LISBURN	ANTRIM	DOWN	
LISMORE	CORK	WATERFORD	
LISNASKEA	FERMANAGH		
LISTOWEL	KERRY		
LONDONDERRY	DONEGAL	LONDONDERRY	

POOR LAW UNION NAME	COUNTIES		
LONGFORD	LONGFORD		
LOUGHREA	GALWAY		
LOWTHERSTOWN/ IRVINESTOWN	FERMANAGH	TYRONE	
LURGAN	ANTRIM	ARMAGH	DOWN
MACROOM	CORK		
MAGHERAFELT	LONDONDERRY		
MALLOW	CORK		
MANORHAMILTON	LEITRIM		
MIDDLETON	CORK		
MILFORD	DONEGAL		
MILLSTREET	CORK		
MITCHELSTOWN	CORK	LIMERICK	
MOHILL	LEITRIM		
MONAGHAN	MONAGHAN		
MOUNTBELLEW	GALWAY		
MOUNTMELLICK	KING'S COUNTY	QUEEN'S COUNTY	
MULLINGAR	WESTMEATH		
NAAS	DUBLIN	KILDARE	WICKLOW
NAVAN	MEATH		
NENAGH	TIPPERARY		
NEW ROSS	CARLOW	KILKENNY	WEXFORD
NEWCASTLE	LIMERICK		
NEWPORT	MAYO		
NEWRY	ARMAGH	DOWN	
NEWTOWNARDS	DOWN		
NEWTOWNLIMAVADY	LONDONDERRY		
OLDCASTLE	CAVAN	MEATH	
OMAGH	TYRONE		
OUGHTERARD	GALWAY	MAYO	
PARSONSTOWN/BIRR	KING'S COUNTY	TIPPERARY	
PORTUMNA	GALWAY		
RATHDOWN	DUBLIN	WICKLOW	
RATHDRUM	WICKLOW		
RATHKEALE	LIMERICK		
ROSCOMMON	GALWAY	ROSCOMMON	
ROSCREA	KING'S COUNTY	QUEEN'S COUNTY	TIPPERARY

POOR LAW UNION NAME	COUNTIES		
SCARRIFF	CLARE	GALWAY	
SHILLELAGH	CARLOW	WEXFORD	WICKLOW
SKIBBEREEN	CORK		
SKULL	CORK		
SLIGO	SLIGO		
STRABANE	DONEGAL	TYRONE	
STRANORLAR	DONEGAL		
STROKESTOWN	ROSCOMMON		
SWINEFORD	MAYO	ROSCOMMON	
THOMASTOWN	KILKENNY		
THURLES	TIPPERARY		
TIPPERARY	LIMERICK	TIPPERARY	
TOBERCURRY	SLIGO		
TRALEE	KERRY		
TRIM	MEATH		
TUAM	GALWAY		
TULLA	CLARE		
TULLAMORE	KING'S COUNTY	WESTMEATH	
URLINGFORD	KILKENNY	TIPPERARY	
WATERFORD	KILKENNY	WATERFORD	
WESTPORT	MAYO		
WEXFORD	WEXFORD		
YOUGHAL	CORK	WATERFORD	

APPENDIX V. ADJUSTMENTS TO COUNTY AFFILIATIONS OF POOR LAW UNIONS BETWEEN THE 1851 AND 1911 CENSUSES

POOR LAW UNION	1851–71	1881	1891	1901	1911
Carlow	Carlow Kildare Queen's Co.	Carlow Queen's Co.	Carlow Queen's Co.	Carlow Queen's Co.	Carlow Queen's Co.
Enniscorthy	Carlow Wexford	Carlow Wexford	Carlow Wexford	Wexford	Wexford
Shillelagh	Carlow Wexford Wicklow	Carlow Wexford Wicklow	Carlow Wexford Wicklow	Wicklow	Wicklow
Celbridge	Dublin Kildare Meath	Dublin Kildare Meath	Dublin Kildare Meath	Dublin Kildare	Dublin Kildare
Naas	Dublin Kildare Wicklow	Kildare Wicklow	Kildare Wicklow	Kildare Wicklow	Kildare Wicklow
Parsonstown	King's Co. Tipperary	King's Co. Tipperary	King's Co. Tipperary	Renamed BIRR PLU	
Birr				King's Co. Tipperary	King's Co. Tipperary
Dundalk	Louth Armagh Monaghan	Louth Armagh Monaghan	Louth Armagh Monaghan	Louth	Louth
Kells	Meath Cavan	Meath Cavan	Meath Cavan	Meath	Meath
[Castletown] devlin called Devlin from 1861 onwards	Meath Westmeath	Westmeath	Westmeath	Westmeath	Westmeath
Dunshaughlin	Meath Dublin	Meath Dublin	Meath Dublin	Meath	Meath

POOR LAW UNION	1851–71	1881	1891	1901	1911
Donaghmore	Queen's Co.	Queen's Co.	Merged into Roscrea & Abbeyleix unions		
Gort	Clare Galway	Galway	Galway	Galway	Galway
Scarriff	Clare Galway	Clare Galway	Clare Galway	Clare	Clare
Tulla	Clare	Clare	Clare	Clare	Merged into Scarriff
Kanturk	Cork Limerick	Cork	Cork	Cork	Cork
Lismore	Cork Waterford	Waterford	Waterford	Waterford	Waterford
Listowel	Kerry	Kerry	Kerry	Kerry Limerick	Kerry Limerick
Glin	Kerry Limerick	Kerry Limerick	Kerry Limerick	Merged into Rathkeale & Listowel unions	
Clogheen	Tipperary Waterford	Tipperary	Tipperary	Tipperary	Tipperary
Ballymoney	Antrim Londonderry	Antrim Londonderry	Antrim Londonderry	Antrim	Antrim
Coleraine	Antrim Londonderry	Antrim Londonderry	Antrim Londonderry	Londonderry	Londonderry
Armagh	Armagh Tyrone	Armagh Tyrone	Armagh Tyrone	Armagh	Armagh
Enniskillen	Cavan Fermanagh Tyrone	Cavan Fermanagh Tyrone	Cavan Fermanagh Tyrone	Cavan Fermanagh	Cavan Fermanagh
Clogher	Monaghan Tyrone	Monaghan Tyrone	Monaghan Tyrone	Tyrone	Tyrone

POOR LAW UNION	1851–71	1881	1891	1901	1911
Gortin	Tyrone	Tyrone	Merged into Omagh		
Ballinrobe	Galway Mayo	Galway Mayo	Galway Mayo	Mayo	Mayo
Clifden	Galway Mayo	Galway	Galway	Galway	Galway
Glennamaddy	Galway Roscommon	Galway	Galway	Galway	Galway
Oughterard	Galway Mayo	Galway	Galway	Galway	Galway
Roscommon	Galway Roscommon	Galway Roscommon	Galway Roscommon	Roscommon	Roscommon
Ballina	Mayo Sligo	Mayo Sligo	Mayo Sligo	Mayo	Mayo
Castlereagh	Mayo Roscommon	Mayo Roscommon	Mayo Roscommon	Roscommon	Roscommon
Newport	Mayo	Mayo	Merged into Westport		
Swineford	Mayo Roscommon	Mayo	Mayo	Mayo	Mayo

APPENDIX VI. COUNTY ELECTORAL DIVISIONS OF IRELAND, 1901 AND 1911

COUNTIES	COUNTY ELECTORAL DIVISIONS		
GALWAY	AHASCRAGH	GLENNAMADDY	ORANMORE
	ATHENRY	GORT	OUGHTERARD
	BALLINASLOE	HEADFORD	PORTUMNA
	CLIFDEN	LETTERMORE	ROUNDSTONE
	DUNMORE	LOUGHREA	SPIDDLE
	GALWAY RURAL	MILLTOWN	TUAM
	GALWAY URBAN	MOUNT BELLEW	
LEITRIM	AGHACASHEL	DRUMSHANBO	MELVIN
	BALLINAMORE	DRUMSNA	MOHILL
	CARRICK-ON-SHANNON	KILTYCLOGHER	NEWTOWNGORE
	CARRIGALLEN	KINLOUGH	RIVERSTOWN
	CLOONE	LURGANBOY	ROOSKY
	DRUMAHAIRE	MAHANAGH	
	DRUMKEERAN	MANORHAMILTON	
MAYO	ACHILL	BELMULLET	KILTAMAGH
	ARDNAREE	CASTLEBAR	LOUISBURGH
	BALLA	CLAREMORRIS	MOUNTFALCON
	BALLINA	CONG	NEWPORT
	BALLINROBE	CROSSMOLINA	PORTROYAL
	BALLYHAUNIS	KILBEAGH	SWINEFORD
	BANGOR	KILKELLY	URLAUR
	BELLAVARY	KILLALA	WESTPORT
ROSCOMMON	ATHLEAGUE	CALTRAGH	KILGLASS
	AUGHRIM	CASTLEPLUNKET	KILTOOM
	BALLAGHADERREEN	CASTLEREA	LOUGHGLINN
	BALLINLOUGH	CLOONFOWER	ROCKINGHAM
	BALLYFERNAN	CREAGH	ROSCOMMON
	BELLANAGARE	ELPHIN	STROKESTOWN
	BOYLE	FRENCHPARK	
SLIGO	ACLARE	COOLAVIN	LISSADILL

COUNTIES	COUNTY ELECTORAL DIVISIONS		
	BALLYMOTE	DROMORE	OWENMORE
	BALLYSADARE	DRUMCLIFF	SLIGO
	BANADA	EASKY	TEMPLEVANNY
	CASTLECONOR	KILMACOWEN/ KILMACKOWEN	TOBERCURRY
	CLIFFONY	KILMACTRANNY	
	COLLOONEY	KILSHALVY	
CARLOW	BAGENALSTOWN	CLONEGALL	MYSHALL
	BALLON	CORRIES	NURNEY
	BALLYMURPHY	GLYNN	OLDLEIGHLIN
	BORRIS	GRANGEFORD	RATHVILLY
	BURTON HALL	HACKETSTOWNS	TULLOW
	CARLOW	LEIGHLINBRIDGE	TULLOWBEG
DUBLIN	BALBRIGGAN	DRUMCONDRA (PART) 1901	PEMBROKE WEST
	BLACKROCK	DUNDRUM	RATHCOOLE
	CASTLEKNOCK	HOWTH (PART) 1901	RATHFARNHAM
	CLONDALKIN (1911)	KINGSTOWN	RATHMINES EAST
	COOLOCK	LUCAN	RATHMINES WEST
	DALKEY	LUSK	STILLORGAN
	DONNYBROOK	NEW KILMAINHAM (1901)	SWORDS
KILDARE	ATHY	CLANE	MAYNOOTH
	BALLITORE	HARRISTOWN	MONASTEREVIN
	BALLYMORE EUSTACE	KILCOCK	MORRISTOWNBILLER
	CARBURY	KILCULLEN	NAAS
	CASTLEDERMOT	KILDARE	NEWBRIDGE
	CELBRIDGE	KILMEAGE	RATHANGAN
	CHURCHTOWN	KILTEEL	TIMAHOE
KILKENNY	BALLYRAGGET	GOWRAN	LISTERLIN
	CALLAN	GRAIGUENAMANAGH	MOTHELL
	CASTLECOMER	INISTIOGE	PILLTOWN
	DUNKITT	KILKENNY RURAL	POLLRONE
	FIDDOWN	KILKENNY URBAN	THOMASTOWN
	FRESHFORD	KNOCKTOPHER	URLINGFORD

COUNTIES	COUNTY ELECTORAL DIVISIONS		
KING'S COUNTY	BALLYBURLEY	DUNKERRIN	KINNITTY
	BALLYCUMBER	EDENDERRY	PHILIPSTOWN
	BANAGHER	EGLISH	PORTARLINGTON NORTH
	BIRR/ PARSONSTOWN	FERBANE	RAHAN
	CLARA	FRANKFORD	SHANNONBRIDGE
	CLONBULLOGE	GEASHILL	SHINRONE
	CLONMACNOISE	KILLEIGH	TULLAMORE
LONGFORD	ABBEYLARA	CLOONEE	LEDWITHSTOWN
	ARDAGH WEST	COLUMBKILLE	LONGFORD
	BALLINALEE	DALYSTOWN	MOYDOW
	BALLINAMUCK	DRUMLISH	MOYNE
	BALLYMAHON	EDGEWORTHSTOWN	NEWTOWN FORBES
	BUNLAHY	FORGNEY	RATHCLINE
	CLOONDARA	GRANARD	
LOUTH	ARDEE	DROGHEDA	LOUTH
	BARRONSTOWN	DROMISKIN	MONASTERBOICE
	CARLINGFORD	DRUMMULLAGH	MULLARY
	CASTLEBELLINGHAM	DUNDALK RURAL	RATHCORR
	CASTLETOWN	DUNDALK URBAN	RAVENDALE
	CLOGHER	DUNLEER	TERMONFECKIN
	CLONKEEN	FAUGHART	
MEATH	ARDBRACCAN	DULEEK	NAVAN
	ATHBOY	DUNBOYNE	NOBBER
	BALLYBOGGAN	DUNSHAUGHLIN	OLDCASTLE
	BECTIVE	INNFIELD	SLANE
	CROSSAKEEL	KELLS	STAMULLEN
	DONAGHPATRICK	KILDALKEY	TARA
	DRUMCONDRA	MOYNALTY	TRIM
QUEEN'S COUNTY	ABBEYLEIX	CULLENAGH	NEWTOWN O'MORESFOREST
	ARLESS	DONAGHMORE	
	BALLINAKILL	DURROW	PORTARLINGTOWN SOUTH
	BALLYBRITTAS	EMO	RATHDOWEY

COUNTIES	COUNTY ELECTORAL DIVISIONS		
	BORRIS-IN-OSSORY	LUGGACURREN	STRADBALLY
	CASTLETOWN	MARYBOROUGH	TINNAHINCH
	CLONASLEE	MOUNTMELLICK	
	COOLRAIN	MOUNTRATH	
WESTMEATH	ATHLONE	FINNEA	MOYDRUM
	AUBURN	KILBEGGAN	MULLINGAR
	BALLYMORE	KILLUCAN	OWEL
	BELVIDERE	KINNEGAD	RAHARNEY
	CASTLETOWN	KINTURK	RATHCONRATH
	COOLE	MILLTOWN	RATHOWEN
	DELVIN	MOATE	
	DRUMRANEY	MOUNT TEMPLE	
WEXFORD	BALLYHUSKARD	FETHARD	NEWTOWNBARRY
	BANNOW	GOREY	OLD ROSS
	BRIDGETOWN	KILLURIN	ROSSLARE
	COOLGREANY	KILTEALY	TAGHMON
	ENNISCORTHY	MONAMOLIN	TINTERN
	FERNS	NEW ROSS	WEXFORD
WICKLOW	ARKLOW	DUNLAVIN	RATHDANGAN
	BALLYARTHUR	GLENDALOUGH	RATHDRUM
	BALTINGLASS	GLENEADY	SHILLELAGH
	BLESSINGTON	HOLLYWOOD	TINAHELY
	BRAY	NEWCASTLE	WICKLOW
	CARNEW	OVOCA	
	DELGANY	POWERSCOURT	
CLARE	BALLYNACALLY	DYSERT	KILLALOE
	CLAREABBEY	ENNIS	KILRUSH
	COOLREAGH	ENNISTIMON	LISDOONVARNA
	COORACLARE	FEAKLE	MILLTOWNMALBAY
	CORROFIN	KILKEE	MOYARTA
	CRUSHEEN	KILKISHEN	QUIN
	DOONBEG	KILLADYSERT	

COUNTIES	COUNTY ELECTORAL DIVISIONS		
CORK	BALLINCOLLIG	CLONKILTY	MONKSTOWN
	BALLYDEHOB	CLOYNE	NEWMARKET
	BALLYHOOLY	DUNMANWAY	QUEENSTOWN
	BANDON	FERMOY	ROSSCARBERY
	BANTEER	INCHIGEELAGH	SKIBBEREEN
	BANTRY	KANTURK	SKULL
	BERE	KINSALE	TIMOLEAGUE
	BLACKROCK	MACROOM	WARRENSCOURT
	BLARNEY	MALLOW	WATERGRASSHILL
	BOHERBOY	MIDLETON	YOUGHAL
	CHARLEVILLE	MITCHELSTOWN	
KERRY	AGHADOE	HEADFORT	MILLTOWN
	ARDFERT	KENMARE	SCARTAGLIN
	BALLYHEIGE	KILGOBBAN	SNEEM
	CAHER	KILLARNEY	TARBERT
	CASTLEGREGORY	KILLORGLIN	TRALEE
	CASTLEISLAND	LISSELTON	VALENTIA
	DINGLE	LISTOWEL	
	GLANBEHY	LIXNAW	
LIMERICK	ABBEYFEALE	CASTLECONNELL	MONAGAY
	ASKEATON	CROOM	NEWCASTLE
	BALLINGARRY	DRUMCOLLIHER	OOLA
	BALLYLANDERS	GLIN	PATRICKSWELL
	BRUFF	HOSPITAL	RATHKEALE
	BRUEE	KILFINNANE	ROXBOROUGH
	CAPPAMORE	KILMALLOCK	
TIPPERARY	ABINGTON	CLOUGHJORDON	NENAGH
(NORTH	ARDCRONY	DERRYCASTLE	NEWPORT
RIDING)	BALLYNACLOGH	HOLYCROSS	ROSCREA
	BIRDHILL	LATTERAGH	TEMPLEMORE
	BORRISOKANE	LITTLETON	TEMPLETOUHY
	BORRISOLEIGH	LORRHA	THURLES
	BOURNEY	MOYALIFF	

COUNTIES	COUNTY ELECTORAL DIVISIONS		
(SOUTH RIDING)	ARDFINNAN	CASHEL	KILLENAULE
	ARDMOYLE/ ARDMAYLE	CLONBEG	KILPATRICK
	BALLYKISTEEN	CLOGHEEN	KILSHEELAN/ KILLSHEELAN
	BALLYPOREEN	CLONMEL	MULLINAHONE
	BANSHA	EMLY	TIPPERARY
	CAHER	FENNOR	TULLAMAIN
	CAPPAGH	FETHARD	
	CARRICK-ON-SUIR	GARRANGIBBON	
WATERFORD	ARDMORE	DUNGARVAN	MODELLIGO
	BALLYDUFF	KILBARRY	PORTLAW
	BALLNAKILL	KILMACTHOMAS	RATHGORMUCK
	CAPPOQUIN	KILMEADAN	RINGVILLE
	CASHMORE	KILRONAN	TALLOW
	CLONEA	KNOCKMAHON	TRAMORE
	DROMANA	LISMORE	
ANTRIM	AHOGHILL	CARRICKFERGUS	KELLS
	ANTRIM	CRUMLIN	KILLOQUIN
	BALLINDERRY	CUSHINDALL	LARNE
	BALLYCASTLE	DERVOCK	LISBURN
	BALLYCLARE	GALGORM	PORTRUSH
	BALLYMENA	GLENARM	RANDLESTOWN
	BALLYMONEY	ISLAND MAGEE	WHITEHOUSE
ARMAGH	ANNAGHMORE	FORKHILL	MIDDLETOWN
	ARMAGH	HAMILTOWN'S BAWN	MONTIAGHS
	CAMLOUGH	KEADY	NEWTOWN-HAMILTON
	CHARLEMONT	KERNAN	PORTADOWN
	CROSSMAGLEN	KILLEVY	POYNTZ PASS
	CROSSMORE	LURGAN	RICH HILL
	DRUMCREE	MARKETHILL	TANDERAGEE
CAVAN	ARVAGH	BELTURBET	KINGSCOURT
	BAILIEBOROUGH	CAVAN	LARAH

COUNTIES	COUNTY ELECTORAL DIVISIONS		
	BALLYCONNELL	COOTEHILL	SHERCOCK
	BALLYJAMESDUFF	DOWRA	STRADONE
	BALLYHAISE	KILLASHANDRA	SWANLINBAR
	BALLYMACHUGH	KILLINKERE	VIRGINIA
	BELLANANAGH	KILNALECK	
DONEGAL	ANNAGARRY	DONEGAL	MILFORD/MILLFORD
	BALLYSHANNON	DUNFANAGHY	MOVILLE
	BUNCRANA	DUNGLOW	PETTIGOE
	BURT	DUNKINEELY	RAPHOE
	CARNDONAGH	GLENTIES	RATHMULLEN
	CASTLE FINN	KILLYBEGS	STRANORLAR
	CHURCH HILL	LETTERKENNY	
DOWN	BALLYNAHINCH	DROMORE	NEWRY
	BANGOR	GARVEAGH	NEWTOWNARDS
	BANBRIDGE	GILFORD	PORTAFERRY
	BRYANSFORD	HILLSBOROUGH	RATHFRYLAND/ RATHFRILAND
	CASTLEWELLAN	HOLYWOOD	SAINTFIELD
	COMBER	KILKEEL	WARRENPOINT
	DOWNPATRICK	KILLYLEAGH	
FERMANAGH	BELLEEK	GARRISON	LISNASKEA
	CROSS	INISHMACSAINT	MAGHERAVEELY
	CRUM	IRVINESTOWN	MAGUIRESBRIDGE
	DERRYLEA	KESH	MONEA
	DERRYLESTER	LECK	NEWTOWNBUTLER
	ENNISKILLEN	LARAGH	ROSSLEA
	FLORENCE COURT	LISBELLAW	
LONDON- DERRY	AGHADOWEY	DUNGIVEN	MAGHERA
	ARTICLAVE	FEENY	MAGHERAFELT
	BALLYKELLY	GARVAGH	MONEYMORE
	BELLAGHY	GLENDERMOT	PORTSTEWART
	CASTLEDAWSON	KILREA	TOBERMORE

COUNTIES	COUNTY ELECTORAL DIVISIONS		
	COLERAINE	LIBERTIES	
	DRAPERSTOWN	LIMAVADY	
MONAGHAN	AGHABOG	CLONTIBRET	KILLEEVAN
	BALLYBAY	CREEVE	LOUGHFEA
	BELLATRAIN	CREMARTIN	MONAGHAN
	BROOMFIELD	DRUM	NEWBLISS
	CARRICKMACROSS	EMYVALE	SCOTSTOWN
	CASTLEBLAYNEY	GLASLOUGH	TEDAVNET
	CLONES	INISHKEEN	
TYRONE	AUGHNACLOY	DRUMQUIN	POMEROY
	BALLYGAWLEY	DUNGANNON	PLUMBRIDGE
	CASTLECAULFIELD	DUNNAMANAGH	SIXMILECROSS
	CASTLEDERG	FINTONA	STEWARTSTOWN
	CLOGHER	MOY	STRABANE
	COAGH	NEWTOWNSTEWART	TRILLICK
	COOKSTOWN	OMAGH	

APPENDIX VII. URBAN AND RURAL DISTRICTS, 1901 AND 1911

COUNTY	COUNTY DISTRICTS
GALWAY	BALLINASLOE URBAN COUNTY DISTRICT
	GALWAY URBAN COUNTY DISTRICT
	BALLINASLOE NO. 1 RURAL DISTRICT
	CLIFDEN RURAL COUNTY DISTRICT
	GALWAY RURAL COUNTY DISTRICT
	GLENNAMADDY RURAL COUNTY DISTRICT
	GORT RURAL COUNTY DISTRICT
	LOUGHREA RURAL COUNTY DISTRICT
	MOUNT BELLEW RURAL COUNTY DISTRICT
	OUGHTERARD RURAL COUNTY DISTRICT
	PORTUMNA RURAL COUNTY DISTRICT
	TUAM RURAL COUNTY DISTRICT
LEITRIM	BALLYSHANNON NO. 3 RURAL COUNTY DISTRICT (1901) *BECAME* KINLOUGH RURAL COUNTY DISTRICT (1911)
	BAWNBOY NO. 2 RURAL COUNTY DISTRICT (1901) *BECAME* BALLINAMORE RURAL COUNTY DISTRICT (1911)
	CARRICK-ON-SHANNON NO. 1 RURAL COUNTY DISTRICT
	MANORHAMILTON RURAL COUNTY DISTRICT
	MOHILL RURAL COUNTY DISTRICT
MAYO	BALLINA URBAN COUNTY DISTRICT
	CASTLEBAR URBAN COUNTY DISTRICT
	WESTPORT URBAN COUNTY DISTRICT
	BALLINA RURAL COUNTY DISTRICT
	BALLINROBE RURAL COUNTY DISTRICT
	BELMULLET RURAL COUNTY DISTRICT
	CASTLEBAR RURAL COUNTY DISTRICT
	CLAREMORRIS RURAL COUNTY DISTRICT
	KILLALA RURAL COUNTY DISTRICT
	SWINEFORD RURAL COUNTY DISTRICT
	WESTPORT RURAL COUNTY DISTRICT
ROSCOMMON	ATHLONE NO. 2 RURAL COUNTY DISTRICT
	BALLINSLOE NO. 2 RURAL COUNTY DISTRICT
	BOYLE NO. 1 RURAL COUNTY DISTRICT
	CARRICK-ON-SHANNON NO. 2 RURAL COUNTY DISTRICT

COUNTY	COUNTY DISTRICTS
	CASTLEREAGH RURAL COUNTY DISTRICT
	ROSCOMMON RURAL COUNTY DISTRICT
	STROKESTOWN RURAL COUNTY DISTRICT
SLIGO	SLIGO URBAN COUNTY DISTRICT
	BOYLE NO. 2 RURAL COUNTY DISTRICT
	DROMORE WEST RURAL COUNTY DISTRICT
	SLIGO RURAL COUNTY DISTRICT
	TOBERCURRY RURAL COUNTY DISTRICT
CARLOW	CARLOW URBAN COUNTY DISTRICT
	BALTINGLASS NO. 2 RURAL COUNTY DISTRICT
	CARLOW NO. 1 RURAL COUNTY DISTRICT (1901) *BECAME* CARLOW RURAL COUNTY DISTRICT (1911)
	NEW ROSS NO. 3 RURAL COUNTY DISTRICT (1901) *BECAME* IDRONE RURAL COUNTY DISTRICT (1911)
DUBLIN	BLACKROCK URBAN COUNTY DISTRICT
	DALKEY URBAN COUNTY DISTRICT
	KILLINEY AND BALLYBRACK URBAN COUNTY DISTRICT
	KINGSTOWN URBAN COUNTY DISTRICT
	PEMBROOK URBAN COUNTY DISTRICT
	RATHMINES AND RATHGAR URBAN COUNTY DISTRICT
	BALROTHERY RURAL COUNTY DISTRICT
	CELBRIDGE NO. 2 RURAL COUNTY DISTRICT
	DUBLIN NORTH RURAL COUNTY DISTRICT
	DUBLIN SOUTH RURAL COUNTY DISTRICT
	RATHDOWN NO. 1 RURAL COUNTY DISTRICT
KILDARE	ATHY URBAN COUNTY DISTRICT
	NAAS URBAN COUNTY DISTRICT
	ATHY NO. 1 RURAL COUNTY DISTRICT
	BALTINGLASS NO. 3 RURAL COUNTY DISTRICT
	CELBRIDGE NO. 1 RURAL COUNTY DISTRICT
	EDENDERRY NO. 2 RURAL COUNTY DISTRICT
	NAAS NO. 1 RURAL COUNTY DISTRICT

COUNTY	COUNTY DISTRICTS
KILKENNY	KILKENNY URBAN COUNTY DISTRICT
	CALLAN NO. 1 RURAL COUNTY DISTRICT (1901) *BECAME* CALLAN RURAL COUNTY DISTRICT (1911)
	CARRICK-ON-SUIR NO. 3 RURAL COUNTY DISTRICT
	CASTLECOMER RURAL COUNTY DISTRICT
	KILKENNY RURAL COUNTY DISTRICT
	NEW ROSS NO. 2 RURAL COUNTY DISTRICT (1901) *BECAME* IDA RURAL COUNTY DISTRICT (1911)
	THOMASTOWN RURAL COUNTY DISTRICT
	URLINGFORD NO. 1 RURAL COUNTY DISTRICT
	WATERFORD NO. 2 RURAL COUNTY DISTRICT
KING'S COUNTY	BIRR URBAN COUNTY DISTRICT
	TULLAMORE URBAN COUNTY DISTRICT
	BIRR NO. 1 RURAL COUNTY DISTRICT
	EDENDERRY NO. 1 RURAL COUNTY DISTRICT
	MOUNTMELLICK NO. 2 RURAL COUNTY DISTRICT (1901) *BECAME* CLONYGOWAN RURAL COUNTY DISTRICT (1911)
	ROSCREA NO. 2 RURAL COUNTY DISTRICT
	TULLAMORE NO. 1 RURAL COUNTY DISTRICT (1901) *BECAME* TULLAMORE RURAL COUNTY DISTRICT (1911)
LONGFORD	GRANARD URBAN COUNTY DISTRICT
	LONGFORD URBAN COUNTY DISTRICT
	BALLYMAHON NO. 1 RURAL COUNTY DISTRICT (1901) *BECAME* LOUTH RURAL COUNTY DISTRICT (1911)
	GRANARD NO. 1 RURAL COUNTY DISTRICT
	LONGFORD RURAL COUNTY DISTRICT
LOUTH	DROGHEDA URBAN COUNTY DISTRICT
	DUNDALK URBAN COUNTY DISTRICT
	ARDEE NO. 1 RURAL COUNTY DISTRICT
	DROGHEDA NO. 1 RURAL COUNTY DISTRICT (1901) *BECAME* LOUTH RURAL COUNTY DISTRICT (1911)
	DUNDALK RURAL COUNTY DISTRICT
MEATH	KELLS URBAN COUNTY DISTRICT
	NAVAN URBAN COUNTY DISTRICT
	TRIM URBAN COUNTY DISTRICT
	ARDEE NO. 2 RURAL COUNTY DISTRICT

COUNTY	COUNTY DISTRICTS
	DROGHEDA NO. 2 RURAL COUNTY DISTRICT (1901) *BECAME* MEATH RURAL COUNTY DISTRICT (1911)
	DUNSHAUGHLIN RURAL COUNTY DISTRICT
	EDENDERRY NO. 3 RURAL COUNTY DISTRICT
	KELLS RURAL COUNTY DISTRICT
	NAVAN RURAL COUNTY DISTRICT
	OLDCASTLE NO. 1 RURAL COUNTY DISTRICT (1901) *BECAME* OLDCASTLE RURAL COUNTY DISTRICT (1911)
	TRIM RURAL COUNTY DISTRICT
QUEEN'S COUNTY	ABBEYLEIX RURAL COUNTY DISTRICT
	ATHY NO. 2 RURAL COUNTY DISTRICT
	CARLOW NO. 2 RURAL COUNTY DISTRICT (1901) *BECAME* SLIEVEMARGY RURAL COUNTY DISTRICT (1911)
	MOUNTMELLICK NO. 1 RURAL COUNTY DISTRICT (1901) *BECAME* MOUNTMELLICK RURAL COUNTY DISTRICT (1911)
	ROSCREA NO. 3 RURAL COUNTY DISTRICT
WESTMEATH	ATHLONE URBAN COUNTY DISTRICT
	ATHLONE NO. 1 RURAL COUNTY DISTRICT
	BALLYMAHON NO. 2 RURAL COUNTY DISTRICT (1901) *BECAME* BALLYMORE RURAL COUNTY DISTRICT (1911)
	DELVIN RURAL COUNTY DISTRICT
	GRANARD NO. 3 RURAL COUNTY DISTRICT (1901) *BECAME* COOLE RURAL COUNTY DISTRICT (1911)
	MULLINGAR RURAL COUNTY DISTRICT
	TULLAMORE NO. 2 RURAL COUNTY DISTRICT (1901) *BECAME* KILBEGGAN RURAL COUNTY DISTRICT (1911)
WEXFORD	ENNISCORTHY URBAN COUNTY DISTRICT
	NEW ROSS URBAN COUNTY DISTRICT
	WEXFORD URBAN COUNTY DISTRICT
	ENNISCORTHY RURAL COUNTY DISTRICT
	GOREY RURAL COUNTY DISTRICT
	NEW ROSS NO. 1 RURAL COUNTY DISTRICT (1901) *BECAME* NEW ROSS RURAL COUNTY DISTRICT (1911)
	WEXFORD RURAL COUNTY DISTRICT
WICKLOW	ARKLOW URBAN COUNTY DISTRICT (1911)
	BRAY URBAN COUNTY DISTRICT

COUNTY	COUNTY DISTRICTS
	WICKLOW URBAN COUNTY DISTRICT
	BALTINGLASS NO. 1 RURAL COUNTY DISTRICT
	NAAS NO. 2 RURAL COUNTY DISTRICT
	RATHDOWN NO. 2 RURAL COUNTY DISTRICT
	RATHDRUM RURAL COUNTY DISTRICT
	SHILLELAGH RURAL COUNTY DISTRICT
CLARE	ENNIS URBAN COUNTY DISTRICT
	KILRUSH URBAN COUNTY DISTRICT
	BALLYVAUGHAN RURAL COUNTY DISTRICT
	CORRIFIN RURAL COUNTY DISTRICT
	ENNIS RURAL COUNTY DISTRICT
	ENNISTIMON RURAL COUNTY DISTRICT
	KILLADYSERT RURAL COUNTY DISTRICT
	KILRUSH RURAL COUNTY DISTRICT
	LIMERICK NO. 2 RURAL COUNTY DISTRICT
	SCARRIFF RURAL COUNTY DISTRICT
	TULLA RURAL COUNTY DISTRICT
CORK	CLONAKILTY URBAN COUNTY DISTRICT
	FERMOY URBAN COUNTY DISTRICT
	KINSALE URBAN COUNTY DISTRICT
	MACROOM URBAN COUNTY DISTRICT (1911)
	MALLOW URBAN COUNTY DISTRICT (1911)
	MIDDLETON URBAN COUNTY DISTRICT
	QUEENSTOWN URBAN COUNTY DISTRICT
	SKIBBEREEN URBAN COUNTY DISTRICT
	YOUGHAL URBAN COUNTY DISTRICT
	BANDON RURAL COUNTY DISTRICT
	BANTRY RURAL COUNTY DISTRICT
	CASTLETOWN RURAL COUNTY DISTRICT
	CLONAKILTY RURAL COUNTY DISTRICT
	CORK RURAL COUNTY DISTRICT
	DUNMANWAY RURAL COUNTY DISTRICT
	FERMOY RURAL COUNTY DISTRICT
	KANTURK RURAL COUNTY DISTRICT
	KILMALLOCK NO. 2 RURAL COUNTY DISTRICT (1901) *BECAME* CHARLEVILLE RURAL COUNTY DISTRICT

COUNTY	COUNTY DISTRICTS
	KINSALE RURAL COUNTY DISTRICT
	MACROOM RURAL COUNTY DISTRICT
	MALLOW RURAL COUNTY DISTRICT
	MIDDLETON RURAL COUNTY DISTRICT
	MILLSTREET RURAL COUNTY DISTRICT
	MITCHELSTOWN NO. 1 RURAL COUNTY DISTRICT
	SKIBBEREEN RURAL COUNTY DISTRICT
	SKULL RURAL COUNTY DISTRICT
	YOUGHAL NO. 1 RURAL COUNTY DISTRICT
KERRY	KILLARNEY URBAN COUNTY DISTRICT
	LISTOWEL URBAN COUNTY DISTRICT
	TRALEE URBAN COUNTY DISTRICT
	CAHERSIVEEN/CAHIRSIVEEN RURAL COUNTY DISTRICT
	DINGLE RURAL COUNTY DISTRICT
	KENMARE RURAL COUNTY DISTRICT
	KILLARNEY RURAL COUNTY DISTRICT
	LISTOWEL NO. 1 RURAL COUNTY DISTRICT (1901) *BECAME* LISTOWEL RURAL COUNTY DISTRICT (1911)
	TRALEE RURAL COUNTY DISTRICT
LIMERICK	CROOM RURAL COUNTY DISTRICT
	KILMALLOCK NO. 1 RURAL COUNTY DISTRICT (1901) *BECAME* KILMALLOCK RURAL COUNTY DISTRICT (1911)
	LIMERICK NO. 1 RURAL COUNTY DISTRICT
	LISTOWEL NO. 2 RURAL COUNTY DISTRICT (1901) *BECAME* GLIN RURAL COUNTY DISTRICT (1911)
	MITCHELSTOWN NO. 2 RURAL COUNTY DISTRICT
	NEWCASTLE RURAL COUNTY DISTRICT
	RATHKEALE RURAL COUNTY DISTRICT
	TIPPERARY NO. 2 RURAL COUNTY DISTRICT
TIPPERARY (NORTH) RIDING	NENAGH URBAN COUNTY DISTRICT
	TEMPLEMORE URBAN COUNTY DISTRICT
	THURLES URBAN COUNTY DISTRICT
	BIRR NO. 2 RURAL COUNTY DISTRICT
	BORRISOKANE RURAL COUNTY DISTRICT
	NENAGH RURAL COUNTY DISTRICT
	ROSCREA NO. 1 RURAL COUNTY DISTRICT
	THURLES RURAL COUNTY DISTRICT

COUNTY	COUNTY DISTRICTS
(SOUTH RIDING)	CARRICK-ON-SUIR URBAN COUNTY DISTRICT
	CASHEL URBAN COUNTY DISTRICT
	CLONMEL URBAN COUNTY DISTRICT
	TIPPERARY URBAN COUNTY DISTRICT
	CALLAN NO. 2 RURAL COUNTY DISTRICT (1901) *BECAME* SLIEVARGAGH RURAL COUNTY DISTRICT (1911)
	CARRICK-ON-SUIR NO. 1 RURAL COUNTY DISTRICT
	CASHEL RURAL COUNTY DISTRICT
	CLOGHEEN RURAL COUNTY DISTRICT
	CLONMEL NO. 1 RURAL COUNTY DISTRICT
	TIPPERARY NO. 1 RURAL COUNTY DISTRICT
	URLINGFORD NO. 2 RURAL COUNTY DISTRICT (1901) *BECAME* GORTNAHOE RURAL COUNTY DISTRICT (1911)
WATERFORD	DUNGARVAN URBAN COUNTY DISTRICT
	CARRICK-ON-SUIR NO. 2 RURAL COUNTY DISTRICT
	CLONMEL NO. 2 RURAL COUNTY DISTRICT
	DUNGARVAN RURAL COUNTY DISTRICT
	KILMACTHOMAS RURAL COUNTY DISTRICT
	LISMORE RURAL COUNTY DISTRICT
	WATERFORD NO. 1 RURAL COUNTY DISTRICT
	YOUHGAL NO. 2 RURAL COUNTY DISTRICT
ANTRIM	BALLYCLARE URBAN COUNTY DISTRICT (1911)
	BALLYMENA URBAN COUNTY DISTRICT
	BALLYMONEY URBAN COUNTY DISTRICT
	CARRICKFERGUS URBAN COUNTY DISTRICT
	LARNE URBAN COUNTY DISTRICT
	LISBURN URBAN COUNTY DISTRICT
	PORTRUSH URBAN COUNTY DISTRICT
	ANTRIM RURAL COUNTY DISTRICT
	BALLYCASTLE RURAL COUNTY DISTRICT
	BALLYMENA RURAL COUNTY DISTRICT
	BALLYMONEY RURAL COUNTY DISTRICT
	BELFAST NO. 1 RURAL COUNTY DISTRICT (1901) *BECAME* BELFAST RURAL COUNTY DISTRICT (1911)
	LARNE RURAL COUNTY DISTRICT
	LISBURN NO. 1 RURAL COUNTY DISTRICT (1901) *BECAME* LISBURN RURAL COUNTY DISTRICT (1911)

COUNTY	COUNTY DISTRICTS
	LURGAN NO. 3 RURAL COUNTY DISTRICT (1901) *BECAME* AGHALEE RURAL COUNTY DISTRICT (1911)
ARMAGH	ARMAGH URBAN COUNTY DISTRICT
	KEADY URBAN COUNTY DISTRICT (1911)
	LURGAN URBAN COUNTY DISTRICT
	PORTADOWN URBAN COUNTY DISTRICT
	TANDERAGEE URBAN COUNTY DISTRICT
	ARMAGH RURAL COUNTY DISTRICT
	BANBRIDGE NO. 2 RURAL COUNTY DISTRICT (1901) *BECAME* TANDERAGEE RURAL COUNTY DISTRICT (1911)
	CASTLEBLAYNEY NO. 2 RURAL COUNTY DISTRICT (1901) *BECAME* CROSS-MAGLEN RURAL COUNTY DISTRICT (1911)
	LURGAN NO. 1 RURAL COUNTY DISTRICT (1901) *BECAME* LURGAN RURAL COUNTY DISTRICT (1911)
	NEWRY NO. 2 RURAL COUNTY DISTRICT
CAVAN	BELTURBET URBAN COUNTY DISTRICT
	CAVAN URBAN COUNTY DISTRICT
	COOTEHILL URBAN COUNTY DISTRICT
	BAILIEBOROUGH RURAL COUNTY DISTRICT
	BAWNBOY NO. 1 RURAL COUNTY DISTRICT (1901) *BECAME* BAWNBOY RURAL COUNTY DISTRICT (1911)
	CAVAN RURAL COUNTY DISTRICT
	COOTEHILL NO. 1 RURAL COUNTY DISTRICT
	ENNISKILLEN NO. 2 RURAL COUNTY DISTRICT
	GRANARD NO. 2 RURAL COUNTY DISTRICT (1901) *BECAME* MULLAGHORAN RURAL COUNTY DISTRICT (1911)
	OLDCASTLE NO. 2 RURAL COUNTY DISTRICT (1901) *BECAME* CASTLERAHAN RURAL COUNTY DISTRICT (1911)
DONEGAL	LETTERKENNY URBAN COUNTY DISTRICT
	BALLYSHANNON NO. 1 RURAL COUNTY DISTRICT (1901) *BECAME* BALLYSHANNON RURAL COUNTY DISTRICT (1911)
	DONEGAL RURAL COUNTY DISTRICT
	DUNFANAGHY RURAL COUNTY DISTRICT
	GLENTIES RURAL COUNTY DISTRICT
	INISHOWEN RURAL COUNTY DISTRICT
	LETTERKENNY RURAL COUNTY DISTRICT
	LONDONDERRY NO. 2 RURAL COUNTY DISTRICT
	MILFORD RURAL COUNTY DISTRICT

COUNTY	COUNTY DISTRICTS
	STRABANE NO. 2 RURAL COUNTY DISTRICT
	STRANORLAR RURAL COUNTY DISTRICT
DOWN	BANBRIDGE URBAN COUNTY DISTRICT
	BANGOR URBAN COUNTY DISTRICT
	DONAGHADEE URBAN COUNTY DISTRICT (1911)
	DROMORE URBAN COUNTY DISTRICT
	HOLYWOOD URBAN COUNTY DISTRICT
	NEWCASTLE URBAN COUNTY DISTRICT (1911)
	NEWRY URBAN COUNTY DISTRICT
	NEWTOWNARDS URBAN COUNTY DISTRICT
	WARRENPOINT URBAN COUNTY DISTRICT
	BANBRIDGE NO. 1 RURAL COUNTY DISTRICT (1901) *BECAME* BANBRIDGE RURAL COUNTY DISTRICT (1911)
	BELFAST NO. 2 RURAL COUNTY DISTRICT (1901) *BECAME* CASTLEREAGH RURAL COUNTY DISTRICT (1911)
	DOWNPATRICK RURAL COUNTY DISTRICT
	KILKEEL RURAL COUNTY DISTRICT
	LISBURN NO. 2 RURAL COUNTY DISTRICT (1901) *BECAME* HILLSBOROUGH RURAL COUNTY DISTRICT (1911)
	LURGAN NO. 2 RURAL COUNTY DISTRICT (1901) *BECAME* MOIRA RURAL COUNTY DISTRICT (1911)
	NEWRY NO. 1 RURAL COUNTY DISTRICT
	NEWTOWNARDS RURAL COUNTY DISTRICT
FERMANAGH	ENNISKILLEN URBAN COUNTY DISTRICT
	BALLYSHANNON NO. 2 RURAL COUNTY DISTRICT (1901) *BECAME* BELLEEK RURAL COUNTY DISTRICT (1911)
	CLONES NO. 2 RURAL COUNTY DISTRICT
	ENNISKILLEN NO. 1 RURAL COUNTY DISTRICT (1901) *BECAME* ENNISKILLEN RURAL COUNTY DISTRICT (1911)
	IRVINGSTOWN NO. 1 RURAL COUNTY DISTRICT (1901) *BECAME* IRVINGS-TOWN RURAL COUNTY DISTRICT (1911)
	LISNASKEA RURAL COUNTY DISTRICT
LONDON-DERRY	COLERAINE URBAN COUNTY DISTRICT
	LIMAVADY URBAN COUNTY DISTRICT
	COLERAINE RURAL COUNTY DISTRICT
	LIMAVADY RURAL COUNTY DISTRICT
	LONDONDERRY NO. 1 RURAL COUNTY DISTRICT
	MAGHERAFELT RURAL COUNTY DISTRICT

COUNTY	COUNTY DISTRICTS
MONAGHAN	CARRICKMACROSS URBAN COUNTY DISTRICT
	CASTLEBLAYNEY URBAN COUNTY DISTRICT
	CLONES URBAN COUNTY DISTRICT
	MONAGHAN URBAN COUNTY DISTRICT
	CARRICKMACROSS RURAL COUNTY DISTRICT
	CASTLEBLAYNEY NO. 1 RURAL COUNTY DISTRICT (1901) *BECAME* CASTLEBLAYNEY RURAL COUNTY DISTRICT (1911)
	CLONES NO. 1 RURAL COUNTY DISTRICT
	COOTEHILL NO. 2 RURAL COUNTY DISTRICT
	MONAGHAN RURAL COUNTY DISTRICT
TYRONE	COOKSTOWN URBAN COUNTY DISTRICT
	DUNGANNON URBAN COUNTY DISTRICT
	OMAGH URBAN COUNTY DISTRICT
	STRABANE URBAN COUNTY DISTRICT
	CASTLEDERG RURAL COUNTY DISTRICT
	CLOGHER RURAL COUNTY DISTRICT
	COOKSTOWN RURAL COUNTY DISTRICT
	DUNGANNON RURAL COUNTY DISTRICT
	IRVINESTOWN NO. 2 RURAL COUNTY DISTRICT (1901) *BECAME* TRILLICK RURAL COUNTY DISTRICT (1911)
	OMAGH RURAL COUNTY DISTRICT
	STRABANE NO. 1 RURAL COUNTY DISTRICT

Census survey

Census	Themes	Townland	Parish	Town/village	Barony	County, city & large town	Province	Parliamentary borough	Electoral division	Poor law union or superintendent registrars' district	Registrars' district	Diocese	Petty session	County district	District electoral division	Ireland
1821	**Census of Ireland for 1821**															
	Persons		x	x	x	x	x									x
	Houses		x	x	x	x	x									x
	Occupational groups		x	x	x	x	x									x
	School pupils		x	x	x	x	x									x
	Age cohorts				x	x	x									x
1831	**Census of Ireland for 1831**															
	Area in statute acres					x	x									x
	Houses		x	x	x	x	x									x
	Occupations (family)		x	x	x	x	x									x
	Persons		x	x	x	x	x									x
	No. of males over 20 years		x	x	x	x	x									x
	Occupations (individuals)		x	x	x	x	x									x
	No. of servants, male & female		x	x	x	x	x									x
	No. of males employed in retail trade or handicraft as masters and workmen					x	x									x
1841	**Addenda to the Census of Ireland for 1841 showing the number of houses, families, and persons in the several townlands and towns**															
	Area in statute acres	x	x	x	x											
	Persons	x	x	x	x											
	Housing	x	x	x	x											

1 This survey is to give readers an indication of the spatial units at which many themes are presented in the censuses. Not every table is represented, the number being so great.

Census	Themes	Townland	Parish	Town/village	Barony	County, city & large town	Province	Parliamentary borough	Electoral division	Poor law union or superintendent registrars' district	Registrars' district	Diocese	Petty session	County district	District electoral division	Ireland
1841	**Report of the Commissioners appointed to take the census of Ireland for 1841**															
	Area in statute acres	x	x	x	x	x	x									x
	Persons	x	x	x	x	x	x									x
	Housing number and grade with the number of families living in each grade	x	x	x	x	x	x									x
	Occupations – persons/families	x	x	x	x	x	x									x
	Education	x	x	x	x	x	x									x
	Ages – 1–12 months and yearly thereafter					x	x										x
	Education – literacy & school attendence					x	x										x
	Marriage					x	x										x
	House accommodation – rural & civic					x	x										x
	Occupations of persons above & under 15 years of age					x	x										x
1841	**Special Features**															
	Emigration – birth-places, occupations					x											x
	Emigration to Great Britain, and foreign countries					x											x
	Rural economy – arable, woods, plantations, etc.					x	x										x
	Rural economy – livestock					x	x										x
	Births each year 1832–41 - rural & civic					x	x										x
	Marriages each year 1830–40 in age cohorts					x^2	x										x
	Ages – 1–12 months and 2 to 113 years						x										x
1841	**Report on the tables of deaths**															
	Deaths – City of Dublin – special report DC																
	Deaths each year 1831/2–1841 according to disease					x	x										x

2 Cities of Dublin, Cork and Town of Belfast

Census	Themes	Townland	Parish	Town/village	Barony	County, city & large town	Province	Parliamentary borough	Electoral division	Poor law union or superintendent registrars' district	Registrars' district	Diocese	Petty session	County district	District electoral division	Ireland
	Deaths according to cause – inquests						X									X
	Deaths in various hospitals according to disease					X										X
	Deaths in lunatic asylums according to age & disease															X
	Deaths in hospitals of jails according to disease					X										X
	Deaths in lying-in hospitals according to disease					X										X
	Deaths in hospitals & sanitary institutions, summary															X
51, part vols i–iv																
	Area	X	X	X	X	X				X	X					
	Persons	X	X	X	X	X				X	X					
	Houses	X	X	X	X	X				X	X					
	Poor law valuation	X	X	X	X	X				X	X					
51, part ii	**Returns of agricultural produce in 1851**															
	CROPS:															
	Extent of crops in acres					X	X			X	X					X
	Number of holdings					X	X			X	X					X
	Division of land					X	X			X	X					X
	Poor law valuation					X	X			X	X					X
	Average rate of produce in each year 1847–51					X	X									X
	Extent of tillage in each year 1847–51					X	X									X
	Produce table					X	X			X						X
	Table of extent of land under crops, with an estimate of the quantity of produce					X	X			X						X
	STOCK:															
	Number of holdings				X	X				X						X
	Numbers of stock				X	X				X						X
	Value of stock in each county £					X	X									X

Census	Themes	Townland	Parish	Town/village	Barony	County, city & large town	Province	Parliamentary borough	Electoral division	Poor law union or superintendent registrars' district	Registrars' district	Diocese	Petty session	County district	District electoral division	Ireland
	Classification of holdings and quantity of stock						x									x
	Number of stockholders and quantity of stock for each year 1847–51					x	x									x
1851, part iii	**Report on the status of disease**															
	The deaf and dumb					x	x			x						x
	The blind					x	x			x						x
	The lunatic and idiotic					x	x			x						x
	The lame and decrepit					x	x			x						x
	The sick in workhouses					x	x			x						x
	The sick in hospitals					x	x									x
	The sick in prisons					x	x									x
	The sick in asylums															x
	The sick at home					x	x									x
	The total sick in Ireland					x	x									x
1851, part iv	**Ages and education**															
	Ages in 5 year cohorts from 1–100 years and upwards				x	x	x									x
	Literacy (number & %)					x	x									x
	School attendance					x	x									x
1851, part v, vol. i	**Tables of deaths – I**															
	Receptions and deaths in infirmaries					x	x									x
	Receptions and deaths in fever hospitals					x	x									x
	Receptions and deaths in lying-in hospitals					x										x
	Receptions and deaths in lunatic hospitals					x										x
	Receptions and deaths in prisons					x	x									x
	Executions					x	x									x
	Percentage of deaths by age cohorts					x	x									x
1851, part v, vol. ii	**Tables of deaths – II**															
	Deaths in general hospitals					x										x
	Deaths in infirmaries					x	x									x

Census	Themes	Townland	Parish	Town/village	Barony	County, city & large town	Province	Parliamentary borough	Electoral division	Poor law union or superintendent registrars' district	Registrars' district	Diocese	Petty session	County district	District electoral division	Ireland
	Deaths in fever hospitals					x	x									x
	Deaths in special hospitals – lying-in/lock					x										x
	Deaths in lunatic asylums					x										x
	Deaths in workhouses and workhouse hospitals					x	x			x						x
	Deaths in prison and prison hospitals					x	x									x
	Deaths in charitable institutions					x										x
	Abstract of inquests					x	x									x
	Abstract of violent deaths						x									x
	County & provincial tables of deaths					x	x									x
	Summary tables of Ireland															x
1851, part v	**General Report, with appendix, county tables, miscellaneous tables & index of names of places**															
	Area in statute acres	x	x	x	x	x	x									x
	Persons	x	x	x	x	x	x									x
	Housing number and grade with the number of families living in each grade	x	x	x	x	x	x									x
	Occupations persons/families	x	x	x	x	x	x									x
	Education	x	x	x	x	x	x									x
	Marriage					x	x									x
	Number of houses & grades with one or more families					x	x									x
	Language				x	x	x									x
	Occupation of persons under 15 & 15 and upwards					x	x									x
	Emigration – Birth-places					x										x
	Emigration – Birth-places and occupation					x										x
	Marriages each year 1841–50 in age cohorts					x										x
	Ages – 1–11 months and 1 to 100 years and upwards					x										
1861, part vols i–iv	**Area, population and houses**															
	Area, population, housing and poor law valuation	x	x	x	x	x	x			x	x					x

Census	Themes	Townland	Parish	Town/village	Barony	County, city & large town	Province	Parliamentary borough	Electoral division	Poor law union or superintendent registrars' district	Registrars' district	Diocese	Petty session	County district	District electoral division	Ireland
1861, part ii, vol. i	**Ages and education**															
	Age and literacy – Leinster & Munster	x	x	x	x	x	x*									x
vol. ii	Age and literacy – Ulster & Connaught	x	x	x	x	x	x									x
	Language (whole country)			x	x	x										x
	School/description & attendance (whole country)				x	x										x
1861, part iii, vol. i	**Vital statistics: status of disease**															
	The deaf and dumb				x	x			x							x
	The blind				x	x			x							x
	The lunatic and idiotic				x	x			x							x
	The lame and decrepit				x	x										x
	The inmates in workhouses				x	x			x							x
	The sick in hospitals				x	x										x
	The sick in asylums and charitable institutions				x											x
	The sick in prisons				x	x										x
	The sick at home				x	x										x
	Total sick in Ireland															x
1861, part iii, vol. ii	**Report and tables relating to deaths**															
	Deaths in general hospitals				x											x
	Deaths in infirmaries				x	x										x
	Deaths in fever hospitals				x	x										x
	Deaths in special hospitals – lying-in/lock				x											x
	Deaths in lunatic asylums				x											x
	Deaths in workhouses and workhouse hospitals				x	x			x							x
	Deaths in prisons and prison hospitals				x	x										x
	Deaths in charitable institutions				x											x
	Coroners' inquests				x	x										x
	General mortality provincial & general summaries					x										x

* Data for Leinster and Munster in vol. ii

Census	Themes	Townland	Parish	Town/village	Barony	County, city & large town	Province	Parliamentary borough	Electoral division	Poor law union or superintendent registrars' district	Registrars' district	Diocese	Petty session	County district	District electoral division	Ireland
1861, part iv, vol. i	**Report and tables relating to the religious profession, education and occupations**															
	Religion			x		x	x	x				x				x
	Religion & literacy		x	x	x	x	x	x								x
	Religion & school/college attendence					x	x									x
vol. ii	Religion by occupation						x									x
1861, part v	***General Report*, with appendix, county tables, summary of Ireland and index to place names**															
	Area in statute acres	x	x	x	x	x	x									x
	Persons	x	x	x	x	x	x									x
	Housing number and grade with the number of families living in each grade	x	x	x	x	x	x									x
	Occupations	x	x	x	x	x	x									x
	Religious profession	x	x	x	x	x	x									x
	Education	x	x	x	x	x	x									x
	House accommodation					x	x									x
	Birthplace					x	x									x
	Marriage					x	x									x
	Occupation of inhabitants					x	x									x
1871, part i, vols i–iv	**Area, houses and population; also ages, civil condition, occupations, birthplaces, religion and education of the people**															
	Area in statute acres	x	x	x	x	x	x	x	x	x	x	x		x		x
	Population	x	x	x	x	x	x	x	x	x	x	x		x		x
	Housing	x	x	x	x	x	x	x	x	x	x	x		x		x
	Valuation	x	x	x	x	x	x									
	Housing number and grade with the number of families living in each grade					x	x									x
	No. in principal institutions					x	x			x						x
	No. blind, deaf, dumb, dumb nor deaf, idiots, lunatics, paupers, sick & prisoners in poor law unions					x	x			x						x
	Vessels and persons on board					x	x									x

Census	Themes	Townland	Parish	Town/village	Barony	County, city & large town	Province	Parliamentary borough	Electoral division	Poor law union or superintendent registrars' district	Registrars' district	Diocese	Petty session	County district	District electoral division	Ireland
	Births, marriages & deaths					x	x			x						x
	Ages of the people			x		x	x			x	x					x
	Civil or conjugal condition of the people					x	x			x						x
	Occupations, <20 years & 20 years and over					x	x									x
	Occupation by age, religion and education					x	x									x
	Occupations of people 20 years and upwards									x						
	Occupations of people <20 years & 20 years & upwards			x												
	No. of farmers & farm holdings					x	x			x						x
	Occupiers of land engaged in pursuits besides farming					x	x									x
	Birthplaces of the people					x	x			x						x
	Foreigners					x	x									x
	Blind, deaf and dumb					x	x									x
	Religious profession of the people	x	x			x	x	x								x
	Religious profession and education	x	x			x	x	x								x
	Religious profession and illiteracy	x				x	x									
	No. educational establishments	x				x	x									x
	Language			x		x	x									x
	Emigration					x	x									x
1871, part ii, vol. i	**Vital statistics: status of disease**															
	The deaf and dumb					x	x			x						
	The blind					x	x			x						
	The lunatic and idiotic					x	x			x						
	The lame or decrepit					x	x									
	The inmates of workhouses					x	x			x						
	The sick in hospitals					x	x									
	The inmates of charitable institutions					x	x									
	The inmates of prisons					x	x									
	The inmates of reformatory schools					x	x									
	The sick in their own homes					x	x									x
	General summary of the sick in Ireland															x

Census	Themes	Townland	Parish	Town/village	Barony	County, city & large town	Province	Parliamentary borough	Electoral division	Poor law union or superintendent registrars' district	Registrars' district	Diocese	Petty session	County district	District electoral division	Ireland
vol. ii	**Report and tables relating to deaths**															
	Inquests					x	x									x
	Deaths in hospitals & sanitary institutions															x
	General hospitals					x										x
	Infirmaries					x	x									x
	Fever hospitals					x	x									x
	Special hospitals – lying-in/lock/ophthalmic					x										x
	Special hospitals – naval/military					x	x									x
	Lunatic asylums					x	x									x
	Deaths in workhouses & workhouse hospitals					x	x			x						x
	Deaths in prisons & prison hospitals					x	x									x
	Reformatory schools					x	x									x
	Charitable institutions					x	x									x
	Provincial & general summaries of deaths						x									x
1871, part iii	*General Report,* **with maps, diagrams, summary tables and appendix**															
	Area, housing & population					x	x			x						x
	Inmates in public institutions					x	x									x
	Ages of the people					x	x									x
	Civil or conjugal condition of the people					x	x									x
	Occupations of the people					x*	x*									x†
	Occupiers of land engaged in pursuits besides farming															x
	Religious profession of the people					x	x					x				x
	Religious profession & education of the people					x	x									x
	Education of the people					x	x									x
	No. in education					x	x									x
	No. of days scholars at school					x	x									x
	Miscellaneous tables (old format)					x	x									x
	Emigration					x	x									x

† English and Irish classification of occupations
* Irish 1841 classification of occupations

Census	Themes	Townland	Parish	Town/village	Barony	County, city & large town	Province	Parliamentary borough	Electoral division	Poor law union or superintendent registrars' district	Registrars' district	Diocese	Petty session	County district	District electoral division	Ireland
1881, part i, vols i–iv	**Area, houses and population: also ages, civil or conjugal condition, occupations, birthplaces, religion and education of the people**															
	Area, population, housing & valuation	x	x	x	x	x	x	x	x	x	x		x			
	Housing number and grade with the number of families living in each grade					x	x									
	No. in principal institutions					x	x									
	No. blind, deaf, dumb, idiots, lunatics, paupers, sick etc.					x	x			x						
	Vessels and persons on board					x	x									
	Births, marriages & deaths					x	x			x						
	Ages of the people			x		x	x			x	x					
	Civil or conjugal condition of the people					x	x			x						
	Occupations of the people <20 years & 20 years and over					x	x									
	Occupation by age, religion and education					x	x									
	Occupations of inhabitants 20 years & upwards									x						
	Occupations of inhabitants <20 years & 20 years and over			x												
	Occupiers of land in other pursuits besides farming					x	x									
	Birthplaces of the people					x	x			x						
	Foreigners					x	x									
	Blind, deaf and dumb					x	x									
	Religious professions of the people	x	x			x	x	x								
	Religious professions & education of the people	x	x			x	x	x								
	Religious profession & illiteracy	x				x	x									
	No. educational establishments	x				x	x									
	Language				x	x	x									
	Emigration					x	x									
1881, part ii	*General Report,* **with illustrative maps and diagrams, tables and appendix**															

Census	Themes	Townland	Parish	Town/village	Barony	County, city & large town	Province	Parliamentary borough	Electoral division	Poor law union or superintendent registrars' district	Registrars' district	Diocese	Petty session	County district	District electoral division	Ireland
	First Series – summaries of tables in county books															
	Area, housing & population						x									x
	Housing number and grade with the number of families living in each grade															x
	No. of persons in principal institutions															x
	No. of blind, deaf, dumb, idiots, lunatics, paupers, sick, and prisoners						x									x
	No. of vessels in ports						x									x
	Deaths, births, marriages						x									x
	Ages of the people						x									x
	Civil or conjugal condition of the people															x
	Occupations of the people															x
	Birthplaces of the people						x	x								x
	Foreigners															x
	Occupations of foreigners															x
	Blind, deaf and dumb															x
	Religious profession of the people						x									x
	Religious profession and education of the people						x									x
	Religious profession and illiteracy						x									x
	Irish language						x									x
	No. of educational establishments & No. of scholars						x									x
	Emigration															x
1881, part ii	***General Report: Second Series***															
	Area, and distribution of land					x	x									x
	Area, housing, population MPD, RC, RP			x		x	x			x			x			x
	Housing number and grade with the number of families living in each grade															x
	Land census:															
	No. agricultural holdings/ valuation, population, housing					x	x			x						x
	No. of stockholders and quantity of livestock					x	x									x
	Extent of land under crops					x	x									x

Census	Themes	Townland	Parish	Town/village	Barony	County, city & large town	Province	Parliamentary borough	Electoral division	Poor law union or superintendent registrars' district	Registrars' district	Diocese	Petty session	County district	District electoral division	Ireland
	Ages of the people															x
	Literacy					x	x									x
	Civil or conjugal condition of the people RC, RP					x	x									x
	Occupations of the people DC, DS, DR															x
	Birthplaces of the people					x										x
	Foreigners/Occupations of foreigners															x
	The sick and infirm RC, RP					x	x			x						x
	The sick in infirmaries, hospitals etc.					x	x									x
	The sick in workhouse hospitals					x	x									x
	The blind					x	x			x						x
	The deaf and dumb					x	x									x
	The lunatic and idiotic					x	x									x
	Inmates in public institutions, etc					x	x									x
	Religious profession of the people			x		x	x	x					x			x
	Religious profession & education of the people					x	x									x
	Religious profession & illiteracy					x	x									x
	No. of scholars at educational establishments					x	x									x
	No. of educational establishments															x
	No. taught specified subjects in school/college					x	x									x
	No. days scholars attended school/college					x	x									x
	Irish speaking population					x	x									x
	Emigration					x	x									x
	Miscellaneous tables (old format)					x	x									x
1891, part i, vols i–iv	**Area, houses & population; also ages, civil or conjugal condition, occupations, birthplaces, religion and education of the people**															
	Area, in statute acres/population, housing	x	x	x	x	x	x	x	x	x	x		x			
	Valuation	x	x	x		x	x									
	Housing number and grade with the number of families living in each grade					x	x									

Census	Themes	Townland	Parish	Town/village	Barony	County, city & large town	Province	Parliamentary division/borough	Electoral division	Poor law union or superintendent registrars' district	Registrars' district	Diocese	Petty session	County district	District electoral division	Ireland
	Numbers in principal institutions					x	x									
	Number of blind, deaf & dumb, dumb not deaf, idiots, lunatics, paupers, sick & prisoners					x	x			x						
	Number of vessels in port					x	x									
	Marriages, births and deaths					x	x			x						
	Ages of the people			x		x	x			x	x					
	Civil or conjugal condition of the people					x	x			x						
	Occupations <20 years & 20 years and over					x	x									
	Occupation by age, religion and education					x	x									
	Occupations of inhabitants 20 years & upwards									x						
	Occupations of inhabitants < 20 & 20 years and upwards			x												
	Occupiers of land engaged in pursuits besides farming					x	x									
	Birthplaces of the people					x	x			x						
	Foreigners					x	x									
	Occupation of foreigners					x	x									
	Blind, deaf and dumb					x	x									
	Religious profession of the people	x	x			x	x	x								
	Religious profession & education of the people	x	x			x	x	x								
	Religious profession and illiteracy	x				x	x									
	No. of educational establishments and pupils	x				x	x									
	Irish-speaking population			x		x	x									
	Emigration					x	x									
1891, part ii	***General Report,* with illustrative maps and diagrams, tables and appendix**															
	First Series:summaries of tables in county books															
	Area, housing & population					x									x	
	Housing number and grade with the number of families living in each grade														x	

Census	Themes	Townland	Parish	Town/village	Barony	County, city & large town	Province	Parliamentary division/borough	Electoral division	Poor law union or superintendent registrars' district	Registrars' district	Diocese	Petty session	County district	District electoral division	Ireland
	No. of persons in principal institutions															x
	No. of blind, deaf, dumb, idiots, lunatics, paupers, sick and prisoners						x									x
	Number of vessels in port						x									x
	Deaths births, marriages						x									x
	Ages of the people						x									x
	Civil or conjugal condition of the people															x
	Occupations < 20 years & over 20 year olds															x
	Occupations of the people by age, religion and literacy															x
	Occupiers of land in non-farming pursuits															x
	Birthplaces of the people					x	x									x
	Foreigners															x
	Occupations of foreigners															x
	Blind, deaf & dumb, idiots, lunatics, paupers etc.															x
	Religious profession of the people						x									x
	Religious profession and education						x									x
	Religious profession and illiteracy						x									x
	Irish-speaking population						x									x
	Number of educational establishments and pupils						x									x
	Emigration															x
1891, part ii	**Second Series: special tables for *General Report***															
	Area and distribution of land					x	x									
	Area, housing, population MPD			x		x	x	x		x				x		x
	Housing number and grade with the number of families living in each grade															x
	Land census:															
	No. agricultural holdings/valuation, population, housing					x	x			x						x
	No. of stockholders and quantity of livestock					x	x									x
	Extent of land under crops					x	x									x
	Age of the people															x
	Literacy					x	x									x

Census	Themes	Townland	Parish	Town/village	Barony	County, city & large town	Province	Parliamentary division/borough	Electoral division	Poor law union or superintendent registrars' district	Registrars' district	Diocese	Petty session	County district	District electoral division	Ireland
	Civil or conjugal condition of the people					x	x									x
	Occupations, < 20 years & 20 years and over DC, DS, DR															x
	Birthplaces of the people					x										x
	Foreigners															x
	Occupations of foreigners															x
	Sick and infirm					x	x			x						x
	The sick in infirmaries, hospitals etc.					x	x									x
	The sick in workhouse hospitals					x	x									x
	The blind					x	x			x						x
	The deaf and dumb					x	x									x
	The lunatic and idiotic					x	x									x
	Inmates in public institutions					x	x									x
	Religious profession of the people			x		x	x	x		x		x				x
	Religious profession and education of the people					x	x									x
	Religious profession and illiteracy					x	x									x
	No. attending educational establishments					x	x									x
	No. of educational establishments															x
	No. taught specified subjects in schools					x	x									x
	No. days scholars attended school/college					x	x									x
	Irish-speaking population					x	x									x
	Emigration					x	x									x
	Miscellaneous tables (old format)					x	x									x
1901, part i, vols i–iv	**Area, houses, and population; also ages, civil or conjugal condition, occupations, birthplaces, religion and education of the people in each county, and summary tables for each province**											CED				
	Area, population, houses, valuation	x	x			x	x	x		x	x		x	x	x	
	Housing number and grade with the number of families living in each grade					x	x									
	Tenement accommodation					x	x							x	x	
	Inmates of institutions					x	x									

CED County electoral division

Census	Themes	Townland	Parish	Town/village	Barony	County, city & large town	Province	Parliamentary division/borough	Electoral division	Poor law union or superintendent registrars' district	Registrars' district	Diocese	County electoral division	County district	District electoral division	Ireland
	The blind, deaf and dumb, lunatics, paupers, the sick etc.					x	x			x						
	Vessels & persons on board ship					x	x									
	Births, marriages and deaths					x	x			x						
	Ages of the people			x		x	x			x	x			x		
	Civil or conjugal condition of the people					x	x			x						
	Occupations of the people			x		x	x							x		
	Birthplaces of the people					x	x							x		
	Foreigners					x	x									
	Occupations of foreigners					x	x									
	The blind, deaf and dumb, lunatics, paupers, the sick etc.					x	x									
	Religious profession of the people	x				x	x									
	Age and education of the people			x		x	x	x						x	x	
	Religious profession and education of the people			x		x	x	x						x	x	
	Religious profession and illiteracy					x	x									
	Irish-speaking population					x	x							x		
	Educational establishments and pupil attendance					x	x								x	
	Emigration					x	x									
1901, part ii	**General Report, with illustrative maps, diagrams, tables and appendix**															
	First series: summaries of county books															
	Area, houses and population						x									x
	Housing number and grade with the number of families living in each grade															x
	Tenement accommodation						x									x
	Persons in principal institutions															x
	Blind, deaf and dumb etc.						x									x
	Number of vessels & persons on vessels						x									x
	Marriages, birth and deaths registered in Ireland in the 10 years 1891–1901						x									x
	Ages of the people						x									x
	Civil or conjugal conditions															x
	Occupations of the people, < 20 and 20 years and over															x

Census	Themes	Townland	Parish	Town/village	Barony	County, city & large town	Province	Parliamentary division/borough	Electoral division	Poor law union or superintendent registrars' district	Registrars' district	Diocese	County electoral division	County district	District electoral division	Ireland
	Occupations of the people, age, religion, literacy															x
	Occupiers of land engaged in other pursuits besides farming															x
	Birthplaces of the people					x	x									x
	Foreigners															x
	Occupations of foreigners															x
	Blind, deaf and dumb etc.															x
	Religious profession of the people						x									x
	Ages and education of the people						x									x
	Religious profession & education of the people						x									x
	Irish language						x									x
	No. of educational establishments and pupils						x									x
	Emigration															x
1901, part ii	**Second series: special tables for *General Report***															
	Area and distribution of land					x	x									x
	Population CB					x	x									x
	Area, population & housing MPD			x				x		x						x
	Housing number and grade with the number of families living in each grade															x
	Tenement accommodation CB															
	Land Census: holding value, population and housing					x	x			x						x
	Area in acres of holdings in each rateable class															x
	No. of holdings in each rateable class					x	x									
	Housing class according to rateable value					x	x									x
	Agricultural statistics – crops					x	x									x
	Agricultural statistics – stock					x	x									x
	Ages of the people															x
	Literacy					x	x									x
	Civil or conjugal conditions					x	x									x
	Occupations of the people DC, DR															x

Census	Themes	Townland	Parish	Town/village	Barony	County, city & large town	Province	Parliamentary division borough	Electoral division	Poor law union or super-intendent registrars' district	Registrars' district	Diocese	County electoral division	County district	District electoral division	Ireland
	Birthplaces of the people					x										x
	Foreigners and their occupations															x
	Sick and infirm					x	x			x						x
	The sick in infirmaries, hospitals etc.					x	x									x
	The sick in workhouse hospitals					x	x									x
	The blind					x	x			x						x
	The deaf and dumb					x	x									x
	The lunatic and idiotic					x	x									x
	Inmates in public institutions					x	x									x
	Inmates in prisons															x
	Religious profession of the people			x		x	x	x		x		x				x
	Religious profession & education of the people					x	x									x
	No. of educational establishments and pupils					x	x									x
	No. taught specific subjects					x	x									x
	No. of days scholars attended school/college					x	x									x
	Irish-speaking population					x	x									x
	Emigration					x	x									x
	Miscellaneous tables (old format)					x	x									x
1911, part i, vols i–iv	**Area, houses, and population; also the ages, civil or conjugal condition, occupations, birthplaces, religions and education of the people**															
	Area, houses population, and valuation	x		x		x	x	x		x	x		x	x	x	
	Housing number and grade with the number of families living in each grade					x	x									
	Tenement accommodation					x	x							x	x	
	Inmates of institutions					x	x									
	The blind, deaf and dumb, lunatics, paupers, the sick and prisoners					x	x			x						
	Vessels and persons on board					x	x									
	Marriages, births and deaths					x	x			x						
	Ages of the people			x		x	x			x	x		x			
	Civil or conjugal condition of the people					x	x			x						

Census	Themes	Townland	Parish	Town/village	Barony	County, city & large town	Province	Parliamentary division/borough	Electoral division	Poor law union or superintendent registrars' district	Registrars' district	Diocese	County electoral division	County district	District electoral division	Ireland
	Occupations of the people			x		x	x							x		
	Occupiers of land in other pursuits besides farming					x	x									
	Birthplaces of the people					x	x							x		
	Foreigners					x	x									
	Occupations of foreigners					x	x									
	Blind, deaf and dumb, lunatics, paupers, sick prisoners					x	x									
	Religious profession of the people		x			x	x									
	Education of the people			x		x	x	x						x	x	
	Religious profession and illiteracy					x	x	x						x	x	
	Irish-speaking population					x	x							x	x	
	Pupil attendance					x	x								x	
	Emigration					x	x									
1911, part ii	***General Report*, with tables and appendix**															
	First series: summaries of tables in county books															
	Area, housing, population							x	x							x
	Housing number and grade with the number of families living in each grade															x
	Tenement accommodation					x										x
	Number in principal institutions					x										x
	Blind, deaf, and dumb, etc.					x										x
	Vessels and persons on board					x										x
	Marriages, births and deaths					x										x
	Ages of the people					x										x
	Civil or conjugal conditions																x
	Occupations of the people																x
	Occupiers of land engaged in pursuits besides farming																x
	Birthplaces of the people					x	x										x
	Foreigners																x
	Occupations of foreigners																x
	Blind, deaf and dumb, etc.																x
	Religious profession of the people					x											x
	Education of the people					x											x

Census	Themes	Townland	Parish	Town/village	Barony	County, city & large town	Province	Parliamentary division/borough	Electoral division	Poor law union or superintendent registrars' district	Registrars' district	Diocese	County electoral division	County district	District electoral division	Ireland
	Irish-speaking population						x									x
	No. attending educational establishments						x									x
	Emigration															x
1911, part ii	**Second series: special tables for *General Report***															
	Area and distribution of land					x	x									x
	Area, housing, population MPD, CB			x		x	x	x		x						x
	Housing number and grade with the number of families living in each grade															x
	Tenement accommodation CB															
	Ages of the people															x
	Literacy					x	x									x
	Civil or conjugal conditions					x	x									x
	Occupations of the people DC, DR															x
	Birthplaces of the people					x										x
	Foreigners/ Occupation of foreigners															x
	The sick and infirm					x	x			x						x
	The Sick in infirmaries, hospitals etc.					x	x									x
	The sick in workhouse hospitals					x	x									x
	The blind					x	x			x						x
	The deaf and dumb					x	x									x
	The lunatic and idiotic					x	x									x
	Public institutions – hospitals, workhouses, etc.					x	x									x
	Religious professions of the people			x		x	x	x		x		x				x
	Education of the people					x	x									x
	No. attending educational establishments					x	x									x
	No. taught specified subjects in schools					x	x									x
	No. of days scholars attended school/college					x	x	x								x
	Irish-speaking language					x	x									x
	Emigration					x	x									x
	Miscellaneous tables (old format)					x	x									x

Census	Themes	Townland	Parish	Town/village	Barony	County, city & large town	Province	Parliamentary borough	Electoral division	Poor law union or superintendent registrars' district	Registrars' district	Diocese	County electoral division	County district	District electoral division	Ireland
	Land Census: holding value, population and housing					x	x			x						x
	Area in acres of holdings in each rateable class					x	x									x
	No. of holdings in each rateable class					x	x									x
	Housing class according to rateable value					x	x									x
	Particulars as to marriage CB, DR, BCB															x

BCB   Belfast county borough
CB   County boroughs
DC   Dublin city
DED   District electoral divisions
DS   Dublin suburbs
DR   Dublin registration districts
MPD Metropolitan police division
PLU   Poor law unions
RC   Registration counties
RP   Registration provinces

Bibliography

ACTS OF PARLIAMENT

52 Geo. 3, c. 133, *An Act for taking an account of the population of Ireland, and of the increase or diminution thereof.*

55 Geo. 3, c. 120, *An Act to provide for the taking an account of the population of Ireland, and for ascertaining the increase or diminution thereof.*

1 & 2 Vict., c. 56, *An Act for the more effectual relief of the poor in Ireland.*

3 & 4 Vict., c. 100, *An Act for taking an account of the population of Ireland.*

13 & 14 Vict., c. 44, *An Act for taking an account of the population of Ireland.*

14 & 15 Vict., c. 68, *Medical Charities Act, 1851.*

61 & 62 Vict., c. 2, *Registration (Ireland) Act, 1898.*

61 & 62 Vict., c. 37, *Local Government (Ireland) Act, 1898.*

House of Commons Journal, vol. lxi, 14 April 1806.

CENSUSES OF IRELAND

Abstract of the population of Ireland, ... with a comparative view of the number of houses and inhabitants as taken in 1813, H.C. 1822 (36), xiv.

Abstract of answers and returns, pursuant to act 55 Geo.3, for taking an account of the population of Ireland in 1821, H.C. 1824 (577), xxii.

Abstract of answers and returns under the population acts Ireland: enumeration 1831, H.C. 1833 (634), xxxix.

Report of the Commissioners appointed to take the census of Ireland for the year 1841, H.C. 1843 [504], xxiv.

Addenda to the census of Ireland for the year 1841; showing the number of houses, families, and persons in the several townlands and towns of Ireland (Dublin, 1844).

The census of Ireland for the year 1851
    part i *Showing the area, population and number of houses by townlands and electoral divisions, vol. i, Province of Leinster*, H.C. 1852–3 [1465, 1553, 1481, 1486, 1488, 1492, 1503, 1496, 1502, 1564, 1527, 1544], xci; vol. ii, *Province of Munster*, H.C. 1852–3 [1552, 1550, 1551, 1543, 1554, 1549, 1545, 1546], xci; vol. iii, *Province of Ulster*, H.C. 1852–3 [1565, 1547, 1563, 1567, 1570, 1574, 1571, 1575, 1579], xcii; vol. iv, *Province of Connaught*, H.C. 1852–3 [1557, 1548, 1542, 1555, 1560], xcii.
    part ii *Returns of agricultural produce in 1851*, H.C. 1852–3 [1589], xciii.

part iii *Report on the status of disease*, H.C. 1854 [1765], lviii.

part iv *Report on ages and education*, H.C. 1856 [2053], xxix.

part v *Tables of deaths*, vol i. *Report, tables of pestilences, and analysis of the tables of deaths*, H.C. 1856 [2087–I], xxix; vol ii *containing the tables and index*, H.C. 1856 [2087–II], xxx.

part vi *General report with appendix, county tables, miscellaneous tables, and index to names of places*, H.C. 1856 [2134], xxxi.

Index *General alphabetical index to the townlands and towns, parishes and baronies of Ireland*, H.C. 1862 [2942], li. Also reprinted by Genealogical Pub. Co. (Baltimore, 1986).

Census of Ireland for the year 1861

part i *Showing the area, population and number of houses by townland and electoral divisions*, vol. i, *Province of Leinster*, H.C. 1863 [3204], liv; vol. ii, *Province of Munster*, H.C. 1863 [3204], liv; vol. iii, *Province of Ulster*, H.C. 1863 [3204], lv; vol. iv, *Province of Connaught*, H.C. 1863 [3204], lv.

part ii vol. i, *Report and tables on ages and education*, H.C. 1863 [3204–1], lvi.
vol. ii, *Report and tables on ages and education*, H.C. 1863 [3204–1], lvii.

part iii *Vital Statistics* vol. i, *Report and tables relating to the status of disease* H.C. 1863 [3204–II], lviii.
Vital Statistics vol. ii, *Report and tables relating to deaths* H.C. 1863 [3204–II], lviii.

part iv *Reports and tables relating to the religious professions, education, and occupations of the people*, vol. i, H.C. 1863 [3204–III], lix.
Reports and tables relating to the religious professions, education and occupations of the people, vol. ii, H.C. 1863 [3204–III], lx.

part v *General report, with appendix, county tables, summary of Ireland and index to names of places*, H.C. 1863 [3204–IV], lxi.

Census of Ireland, 1871

part i *Area, houses and population; also the ages, civil condition, occupations, birthplaces, religion and education of the people*, vol. i, *Province of Leinster, with summary tables and index* H.C. 1872 [C. 662–i to xiii], lxvii; vol. ii, *Province of Munster*, H.C. 1873 [C. 873–1 to vii], lxxii; vol. iii, *Province of Ulster*, H.C. 1874 [C. 964–1 to X], lxxiv; vol. iv, *Province Connaught*, H.C. 1874 [C. 1106–1 to VII], lxxiv.

part ii *Vital Statistics*, vol. i, *Report and tables relating to the status of disease*, H.C. 1873 [C. 876], lxxii.
Vital Statistics, vol. ii, *Report and tables relating to deaths*, H.C. 1874 [C. 1000], lxxiv.

part iii *General Report, with illustrative maps and diagrams, summary tables and appendix*, H.C. 1876 [C. 1377], lxxxi.

Index *Alphabetical index to the townlands and towns of Ireland showing number and sheet of barony, parish, poor law union and poor law electoral divisions in which they are situated; and the volume and page in the census of 1871*, H.C. 1877 [C. 1711], lxxxvii.

Census of Ireland, 1881

part i   *Area, houses and population; also the ages, civil or conjugal condition, occupations, birthplaces, religion and education of the people*, vol. i, *Province of Leinster*, H.C. 1881 [C. 3042], xcvii; vol. ii, *Province of Munster*, H.C. 1882 [C. 3148], lxxvii; vol. iii, *Province of Ulster*, H.C. 1882 [C. 3204], lxxviii; vol. iv, *Province of Connaught*, H.C. 1882 [C. 3268], lxxix.

part ii *General Report, with illustrative maps and diagrams, tables and appendix*, H.C. 1882 [C. 3365], lxxvi.

Index *Supplement to the alphabetical index of the townlands and towns of Ireland; with separate indices of the parishes, baronies, poor law unions, and poor law electoral divisions dispensary districts, petty sessions districts and parliamentary boroughs in Ireland in 1871*, H.C. 1882 [C. 3379], lxxix.

Census of Ireland, 1891

part i   *Area, houses and population; also the ages, civil or conjugal condition, occupations, birthplaces, religion and education of the people for each county; with summary tables, and indexes*, vol. i, *Province of Leinster*, H.C. 1890–91 [C. 6515], xcv; vol. ii, *Province of Munster*, H.C. 1892 [C. 6567], xci; vol. iii, *Province of Ulster*, H.C.1892 [C. 6626], xcii; vol. iv, *Province of Connaught*, H.C.1892 [C. 6685], xciii.

part ii *General Report, with illustrative maps and diagrams, tables and appendix*, H.C. 1892 [C. 6780], xc.

Index *Supplement (containing the revisions in townlands etc. up to 5th April 1891) to the Alphabetical index to the townlands and towns of Ireland, showing the number of the sheet of Ordnance Survey maps on which they appear, also the areas of the townlands, the county, barony, parish, poor law union and poor law electoral division etc.* H.C. 1892 [C. 6781], xc.

Census of Ireland, 1901

part i   *Area, houses and population: also the ages, civil or conjugal condition, occupations, birthplaces, religion and education of the people for each county; and summary tables of each province, vol. i, Province of Leinster*, H.C. 1902 [Cd. 847], cxxiii, vol. ii, *Province of Munster*, H.C. 1902 [Cd. 1058], cxxv; vol. iii, *Province of Ulster*, H.C. 1902 [Cd. 1123], cxxvi, cxxvii; vol. iv, *Province of Connaught*, H.C. 1902 [Cd. 1059], cxxviii.

part ii *General Report, with illustrative maps and diagrams, tables and appendix*, H.C. 1902 [Cd. 1190], cxxix.

Index *General topographical index, consisting of an alphabetical index to the townlands and towns of Ireland and indices to the parishes, baronies, poor law unions (or superintendent registrars' districts), district electoral divisions (dispensary or registrars' districts), county districts, county electoral divisions and parliamentary divisions in Ireland;* H.C. 1904 [Cd. 2071], cix.

Census of Ireland, 1911
> part i *showing area, houses and population; also the ages, civil or conjugal condition, occupations, birthplaces, religion and education of the people for each county; and summary tables of each province,* vol. i, *Province of Leinster,* H.C. 1912–13 [Cd. 6049], cxiv; vol. ii, *Province of Munster,* H.C. 1912–13 [Cd. 6050], cxv; vol. iii, *Province of Ulster,* H.C. 1912–13 [Cd. 6051], cxvi; vol. iv, *Province of Connaught,* H.C. 1912–13 [Cd. 6052], cxvii.
> part ii *General Report,* with, tables and appendix, H.C. 1912–13 [Cd. 6663], cxviii.

Index *Supplement to the general topographical index of Ireland, containing all the territorial divisions in which an alteration has been made between 31 March 1901 and 2 April 1911, comprised in the following indices, viz.: alphabetical indices to the Townlands and Towns, district electoral divisions, dispensary (or Registrars') Districts, poor law unions (or superintendent registrar's districts), county districts, and county electoral divisions, together with a reference index to the district electoral divisions of Ireland, giving their index numbers in Tables VII of the county books of the census of 1911, and their numbers in the arrangements followed in the same table in the census books of 1901;* H.C. 1913 [Cd. 6756], lxxx.

Saorstát Éireann, census of population 1926, vol. x: General Report. Dublin, 1934.
Twenty-seventh Annual Report under Local Government Board (Ireland) Act, 35 & 36 Victoria, chap 69, H.C. 1899 [C. 9480], xxxix.
Larcom, Thomas A., 'On Territorial Divisions of Ireland' in *Correspondence relating to the measures adopted for the relief of the distress in Ireland,* Board of Works Series, H.C. 1847 [764], l.

SECONDARY SOURCES

Andrews, J.H., *A paper landscape: the Ordnance Survey in nineteenth-century Ireland* (Oxford, 1975; repr. with new preface, Dublin 2002).
Armstrong, W.A., 'The use of information about occupation' in E.A. Wrigley (ed.), *Nineteenth-century society: essays in the use of quantitative methods* (Cambridge, 1972).
Bourke, Joanne, *Husbandry to housewifery: women, economic change and housework in Ireland, 1890 to 1914* (Oxford, 1993).

Buxton, David, 'The census of the deaf and dumb in 1851', *Journal of the Statistical Society of London*, xviii (1855), pp 174–85.

Clarkson, L.A., Crawford, E. Margaret, Litvack, M.A., *Occupations of Ireland, 1841* (4 vols. Belfast, 1995).

Collins, Peter, *Pathways to Ulster's past: sources and resources for local studies* (Belfast, 1998).

Connell, K.H., *The population of Ireland, 1750 to 1845* (Oxford, 1950).

Connolly, S.J. (ed.), *The Oxford companion to Irish history* (Oxford, 1998).

Crawford, E. Margaret, 'Scurvy in Ireland during the Great Famine', *Journal of the Society for the Social History of Medicine*, i, no. 3 (1988), pp 281–300.

—— 'Subsistence crises and famines in Ireland: a nutritionist's view' in E. Margaret Crawford (ed.), *Famine: the Irish experience, 900–1900: subsistence crises and famines in Ireland* (Edinburgh, 1989), pp 198–219.

—— 'Typhus in Ireland' in G. Jones & E. Malcolm (eds), *Medicine, disease and the state in Ireland, 1650–1940* (Cork, 1999), pp 121–37.

Crawford, W.H. & Foy, R.H. (eds), *Townlands in Ulster: local history studies* (Belfast, 1998).

Crotty, Raymond, *Irish agricultural production* (Cork, 1966).

Dorling, Daniel, *A new social atlas of Britain* (Chichester, 1995).

Duffy, Seán (ed.), *Atlas of Irish history* (Dublin, 1997).

Fitzpatrick, David, 'The disappearance of the Irish agricultural labourer, 1841–1912', *Journal of the Economic and Social History Society of Ireland*, vii (1980), pp 66–92.

Froggatt, P., 'Sir William Wilde and the 1851 Census of Ireland', *Medical History*, ix (1965), pp 302–27.

—— 'The demographic work of Sir William Wilde', *Irish Journal of Medical Science*, vi (1965), pp 213–30.

—— 'Sir William Wilde, 1815–1876', *Proceedings of the Royal Irish Academy*, vol. 77, C, no. 10 (1977), pp 261–78.

—— 'The census in Ireland of 1813–15', *Irish Historical Studies*, xiv, no. 55 (1965), pp 227–35.

Gillespie, Raymond & Hill, Myrtle (eds), *Doing Irish local history: pursuit and practice* (Belfast, 1998).

Grimshaw, Thomas W., *On the methods of drawing up census returns* (Vienna, 1887).

Gurrin, Brian, *Pre-census sources for Irish demography*, Maynooth Research Guides for Irish Local History: number 5 (Dublin, 2002).

Jordan, Thomas E., '"A great statistical operation": a century of Irish censuses, 1812–1911', *New Hibernia Review*, i (1997), pp 94–114.

—— *Ireland's children: quality of life, stress, and child development in the Famine era* (Westport, Connecticut, 1998).

Kennedy, L., Ell, P., Crawford, E. Margaret, Clarkson, L.A., *Mapping the Great Irish Famine* (Dublin, 1999).

Larcom, Thomas, 'Observations on the Census of Ireland in 1841', *Journal of the Statistical Society of London,* vi (1843), pp 323–51.

Laslett, Peter, 'Introduction: the history of the family' in Peter Laslett (ed.), *Household and family in past times* (Cambridge, 1972).

Lee, J.J., 'On the accuracy of the pre-Famine Irish censuses' in J.M. Goldstrom & L.A. Clarkson (eds), *Irish population, economy and society: essays in honour of the late K.H. Connell* (Oxford, 1981), pp 37–56.

Linehan, Thomas P., 'History and development of Irish population censuses', *Journal of the Statistical and Social Inquiry Society of Ireland,* xxvi, part 4 (1991–2), pp 91–125.

——— 'The development of official Irish statistics', *Journal of the Statistical and Social Inquiry Society of Ireland,* xxvii, part 5 (1997–8), pp 47–88.

McDowell, R.B., *The Irish administration, 1801–1914* (London, 1964).

Mokyr, Joel, *Why Ireland starved: a quantitative and analytical history of the Irish economy, 1800–45* (London, 1983).

Nicholls, G., *A history of the Irish poor law* (London, 1856; repr. New York, 1967).

Nolan, William, *Tracing the past: sources for local studies in the Republic of Ireland* (Dublin, 1982).

O'Neill, Kevin, *Family and farm in pre-Famine Ireland: the parish of Killashandra* (Madison, 1984).

Petty, William, *The political anatomy of Ireland* (London 1691; repr. Shannon, 1970).

'Report of Council on Mr Jephson's suggestions as to the census of 1881', *Journal of the Statistical and Social Inquiry Society of Ireland,* viii (1881), pp 158–9.

'Report upon the recent Epidemic Fever in Ireland', *Dublin Quarterly Journal of Medical Science,* vii (1849), pp 64–126, pp 340–404, viii, pp 1–86, pp 270–339.

Thompson, William J., 'The development of the Irish Census', *Journal of the Statistical and Social Inquiry Society of Ireland,* xii (1911), pp 474–88.

Vaughan, W.E. and Fitzpatrick, A.J. (eds), *Irish historical statistics: population, 1821–1971* (Dublin, 1978).

Wilson, T.G., *Victorian doctor: life of Sir William Wilde* (London, 1942).

Woods, Herbert, 'Methods of registering and estimating the population of Ireland before 1864', *Journal of the Statistical and Social Inquiry of Ireland,* xii (1909), pp 219–29.

Young, Arthur, *A tour in Ireland: with general observations on the present state of that kingdom. Made in the years 1776, 1777, and 1778* (2 vols. 2nd ed. London, 1780).